ROME

Elisa Colarossi, Angela Corrias,
Angelo Zinna

Contents

Above Marble busts, Vatican Museums (p100)

FANCY A PIZZA?
You won't have to go far for a slice: Rome has about 15,500 pizza joints within its borders.

The city's province has more pizzerias than any other Italian province.

STREET FOOD
STORIES

Get ready to see your carb intake skyrocket: Rome's food scene will tempt you at literally every street corner. Yes, eating in Italy is all about sitting down and taking the time to enjoy a well-cooked dish, but restaurant meals are simply too far apart to resist a slice of *pizza rossa* (pizza with tomato sauce), a *supplì* (risotto ball) or a gelato on the go.

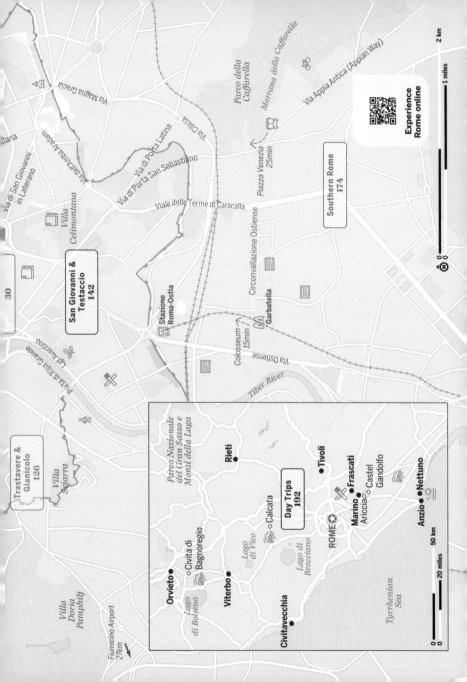

Trastavere & Gianicolo 126

Villa Sciarra

Villa Doria Pamphilj

Flumicino Airport 27km

30

San Giovanni & Testaccio 142

Villa Celimontana

Villa dell'Ariana Acadian

Via di San Giovanni in Laterano

Via Magna Grecia

Porta di Ripa Grande

Lgt Aventino

Via di Porta Latina

Via di Porta San Sebastiano

Viale delle Terme di Caracalla

Via Cilicia

Parco della Caffarella

Marrana della Caffarella

Via Appia Antica (Appian Way)

Piazza Venezia 25min

Southern Rome 174

Circonvallazione Ostiense

Stazione Roma-Ostia

Garbatella

Colosseum 15min

Via Ostiense

Tiber River

Experience Rome online

1 mile

2 km

N

Parco Nazionale del Gran Sasso e Monti della Laga

Rieti

Tivoli

Orvieto

Civita di Bagnoregio

Lago di Bolsena

Viterbo

Calcata

Lago di Vico

Lago di Bracciano

Day Trips 192

ROME

Frascati

Marino

Ariccia

Castel Gandolfo

Anzio

Nettuno

Civitavecchia

Tyrrhenian Sea

20 miles

50 km

▰▰▰ Discover newly opened sections of Rome's most famous archaeological monuments. Explore local markets to get a feel for the city's multicultural character. Step into baroque palaces and majestic cathedrals to admire the work of legendary artists. Stand in awe before the masterpieces of the Vatican. Enjoy a slice of *pizza rossa* as you seek out eye-catching murals in up-and-coming neighbourhoods. Hop from piazza to piazza and take in the elegance of the city's monumental fountains.

This is Rome.

TURN THE PAGE AND START PLANNING YOUR NEXT BEST TRIP →

Villa Ada

Villa Borghese & Northern Rome
158

Via Nomentana

Viale Regina Elena

Via del Ramni

Via Tiburtina

Fumicino Airport
30min

Via Giovanni Giolitti

Via Salaria

Via XX Settembre

Stazione Termini

Monti, Esquilino &
San Lorenzo
112

Via Mer

Via Pinciana

Via Giovanni Lanza

Parco del
Colle Oppio

Colosseum

Villa Borghese

Giardino
del Quirinale

Via Nazionale

Via dei Fori Imperiali

Basilica di
Santa Maria
del Popolo

Spanish
Steps

Roman
Forum

Ancient Rome

Vatican City
40min

Tridente, Trevi &
the Quirinale
74

Piazza
Venezia

Isola
Tiberina

Via Flaminia

Centro Storico
52

Tiber River

Piazza
Navona

Lgt Flaminio

Tiber River

Via Marcantonio Colonna

Via Cola di Rienzo

Via Crescenzio

Tiber River

Giancolo
(Janiculum)

Viale Angelico

Viale delle Milizie

Ottaviano-
San Pietro
Stazione Termini
10min

Vatican City,
Borgo & Prati
96

Parco
della
Vittoria

St. Peter's
Basilica

Villa
Abamelek

→ CACIO E PEPE

Pecorino Romano cheese and freshly ground pepper mix with al dente spaghetti or *tonnarelli* (egg pasta similar in shape to spaghetti but thicker and rougher) to create *cacio e pepe,* Rome's simple, mouthwatering classic dish.

▶ Try it at classic trattoria Felice a Testaccio p155

VLADISLAV CHUSOV/SHUTTERSTOCK ©

ROME BEST EXPERIENCES

Left Pizza slices on the go
Right *Cacio e pepe* **Below** Aperol spritz cocktails

JEWISH DELIGHTS

Rome has had Jewish residents since the 2nd century BCE, and the community has developed a unique cuisine. Try *alla giuda* artichokes, falafel and kosher meat in the Ghetto.

RIGHT VENTDUSUD/SHUTTERSTOCK ©
LEFT DRAGON_FLY/SHUTTERSTOCK ©

↑ APERITIVO, ANYONE?

Fill the gap before the late Italian dinner time with a glass of Castelli Romani wine or a spritz accompanied by local cheeses and cured meats.

▶ Head to Trastevere for a perfect *aperitivo,* or choose a venue in Prati (p103).

Best Food Experiences

▶ Enjoy a slice or two of *pizza rossa* at Panificio Passi in Testaccio (p155)

▶ Sink your teeth into some *torta ricotta e visciole* at the kosher Boccione bakery (p69)

▶ Try classic Roman recipes such as *pollo alla cacciatora* in sandwich form at Trapizzino in Trastevere (p133)

▶ Snack on *supplì* at Supplizio in the Centro Storico (p73)

▶ Take a refreshing gelato break near Vatican City at Neve di Latte (p103)

6

↘ GALLERIES & ARTWORKS

The Vatican Museums comprise 1400 rooms, chapels and galleries.

Despite the available space, less than a third of the Vatican's art collection is currently exhibited.

Best Vatican Art Experiences

▶ Visit the awe-inspiring Sistine Chapel (p101)

▶ See how Ignazio Danti represented the world in the Gallery of Maps (p101)

▶ Enter Raphael's Rooms (pictured above) to admire the work of one of the greatest Renaissance artists (p101)

▶ Marvel at the astonishing sculptures of the Octagonal Court (p101)

GEMS OF THE VATICAN

Covering an area of 44 hectares, the Vatican Museums house a colossal collection of precious artworks gathered over the course of centuries. One of the world's largest museums, it can feel overwhelming: there are approximately 20,000 artworks on display. Take your time to admire canvases and frescoes by some of the greatest names in art history.

PIAZZA
HOPPING

Best Piazza Experiences

▸ **Explore Piazza di Spagna, home of the famous Spanish Steps** (p82)

▸ **Admire the famous basilica from St Peter's Square** (p106)

▸ **Visit the monumental Piazza del Popolo** (p90)

▸ **Eat a sandwich at Trapizzino in Piazza Trilussa** (p133)

▸ **Climb to ancient Rome's Piazza del Campidoglio** (p40)

■■■■ Piazzas are where Rome comes alive. Whether you're looking for markets, nightlife or monumental sculpture, you can be sure the setting will be memorable.

Simply wandering from one square to another – taking in everything from grand open spaces to quiet city corners perfect for a wine break – will create a satisfying itinerary.

TOP: GIVIDIN/SHUTTERSTOCK ©, BOTTOM: ARTUR BOGACKY/SHUTTERSTOCK ©

← PIAZZA NAVONA

The famous Piazza Navona, in the Centro Storico, is built atop the Unesco-listed Stadio di Domiziano. An open-air museum, the square features sculptures, baroque architecture and archeological ruins.

→ PIAZZA DELLA ROTONDA

An Egyptian obelisk stands in the Centro Storico's Piazza della Rotonda. Patronise one of the square's restaurants to eat under the gaze of the Pantheon, formerly a pagan temple.

Above left Piazza Navona
Left Piazza della Rotonda

COLOSSAL CAPACITY

When it was used as a stadium, the Colosseum hosted up to 50,000 spectators.

Today, approximately 21,000 people visit the site daily.

ANCIENT
WONDERS

The Colosseum hardly needs an introduction, but ancient Rome doesn't stop there: the Roman Forum, the Palatine Hill and the Domus Aurea (Emperor Nero's forgotten residence) are just some of the visible traces of Rome's glorious past. Take your time to dive deep into the history of the city's origins and discover newly uncovered sections of Rome's archaeological park.

→ COLOSSEUM, UNDERGROUND

The area beneath the Anfiteatro Flavio, better known as the Colosseum, has recently opened to the public for the first time, offering new insight into Italy's most iconic monument.

▶ Learn more on p38.

Left Colosseum facade **Right** Colosseum interior **Below** Roman Forum

PALATINO: THE ORIGIN STORY

The legend of Rome's foundation starts here, on the Palatine Hill, where Romulus established his kingdom after killing his brother Remus in the 8th century BCE.

↑ THE ROMAN FORUM

Traces of pre-Christian beliefs still dot the Forum's area, amid the remnants of political buildings and massive marble triumphal arches.

Best Archaeological Experiences

▶ Discover the Domus Aurea, Nero's luxurious residence, hidden beneath the Baths of Trajan (p36)

▶ Watch a summertime opera at the 3rd-century Baths of Caracalla (p34)

▶ Visit the Casa delle Vestali (House of the Vestal Virgins) in the Forum, where young girls kept a sacred fire burning (p42)

▶ Admire the ruins of Emperor Domitian's opulent centre of power in the Palatine Hill (p44)

ARCHITECTURAL
OPULENCE

▬▬▬ Once home to aristocratic families, the sumptuous palaces and villas that stand in Rome's centre tell stories of opulence and refined taste. Rare paintings and sculptures collected by the nobility over centuries fill high-ceilinged rooms furnished with baroque decorations and remarkable frescoes, allowing for full immersion into the art and architecture of the past.

Palazzo Altemps
Classical sculpture
Within the inestimable 15th-century Palazzo Altemps, in Piazza Sant' Apollinare, you'll find one of the most intriguing classical sculpture museums in Rome, featuring such masterpieces as the intricate 3rd-century Ludovisi Battle Sarcophagus and a 2nd-century copy of the Greek *Galatian Suicide*.

🚶 right by Piazza Navona ▶ p65

Palazzo Spada
Architectural trickery
In a courtyard of the 16th-century Palazzo Spada an astonishing illusion presents itself. Designed by legendary architect Francesco Borromini in 1653, a 'forced perspective' gallery tricks visitors' eyes into seeing a much longer colonnade than the one that's actually there.

🚶 steps from Campo de' Fiori ▶ p58

Map labels: Giardino del Lago · Il Lago · Viale Pietro Canonica · Piazza di Siena · Viale Fiorello La Guardia · VILLA BORGHESE · Viale del Muro Torto · Villa Medici · Via di Porta Pinciana · Spagna · Via Sistina · CAMPO MARZIO · Via dei Due Macelli · Ponte Cavour · Piazza Cavour · Via Tomacelli · Tiber River · Via del Clementino · Via del Tritone · COLONNA · Ponte Umberto I · Trevi Fountain · Giardino del Quirinale · CENTRO STORICO · Via del Corso · TREVI · PIGNA · Piazza Navona · SANT'EUSTACHIO · Corso Vittorio Emanuele II · Campo de' Fiori · Via Capo di Ferro · Tiber River · L.gt D.Sangallo · Ponte Garibaldi · Isola Tiberina · Via Garibaldi · GIANICOLO · Gianicolo (Janiculum) · TRASTEVERE · Ponte Palatino

Villa Borghese
Masterpieces surrounded by greenery

After a romantic boat ride on the lake in the Villa Borghese Gardens, step into the villa itself to visit the enchanting 17th-century Galleria Borghese. This luxurious mansion turned museum houses master-pieces by Caravaggio and Peter Paul Rubens.

Ⓜ Flaminio or Spagna ▶ p162

SALARIO

Corso Trieste

Via Nomentana

Via Alessandro Torlonia

Villa Torlonia

Via Lazzaro Spallanzani

Piazza Galeno

Villa Torlonia
Neoclassical oasis

A more recent addition to the capital's vast collection of grandiose residences, the 19th-century Villa Torlonia has a distinctively neoclassical style. It's here that Benito Mussolini came to live with his family in 1925 (paying only 1 lira in rent).

Ⓜ Sant'Agnese/Annibaliano ▶ p166

SALLUSTIANO   *Porta Pia*

Via Vittorio Veneto

Palazzo Barberini
Frescoes and baroque architecture

With a grand hall featuring Pietro da Cortona's 530-sq-metre ceiling fresco *Allegory of Divine Providence and Barberini Power,* this 17th-century palazzo houses one of Rome's most impressive art collections.

Ⓜ *Barberini* ▶ p80

Viale del Policlinico

Barberini
Ⓜ
Via Barberini

Via XX Settembre

Via Agostino de Pretis

Piazza dei Cinquecento

Via Marsala

Viale dell' Università

Città Universitaria

Galleria Doria Pamphilj
Renaissance art

With works by Caravaggio, Raphael, Velázquez and Tintoretto, the gallery in this majestic palazzo houses Rome's most precious private collection. Roam its gilded rooms and be inspired by the extraordinary canvases on display.

🚶 *3 min walk from Piazza Venezia* ▶ p63

Via Panisperna

MONTI

Parco di Traiano

Via Merulana

SAN LORENZO

Via Labicana   *Viale Manzoni*   *Via Statilia*

SAN GIOVANNI

🧭 N

0 _____ 500 m
0 _____ 0.25 miles

↘ INDUSTRIAL OSTIENSE

Expanding under the imposing Gazometro, once Europe's largest gasometer, Ostiense has transformed from the industrial core of southern Rome into a thriving creative hub.

STREET-ART
STUNNERS

▬▬▬▬ Not all remarkable paintings are found in museums and galleries, and not all art belongs to the past. Rome's thriving street-art scene spans far and wide, with internationally renowned works to be discovered in the up-and-coming districts of Ostiense, Garbatella and San Lorenzo.

Best Street-Art Experiences

▶ Visit Lorenzo Crudi's colourful Piazza dell' Immacolata in San Lorenzo (p119)

▶ Gaze up at Blu's huge mural in Ostiense (p182)

▶ Admire Iena Cruz' massive ecological artwork, *Hunting Pollution* (pictured above; p183)

▶ Head to Via Passino to check out *Oh My Darling Clementine* by Solo and Diamond (p188)

MONUMENTAL
FOUNTS

Best Fountain Experiences

▶ Visit Giacomo della Porta's Fontana delle Tartarughe (p67)

▶ Explore the Orto Botanico to discover the garden's Le Quattro Fontane (p135)

▶ Marvel at the Piazza di Spagna's Baroque-style Fontana della Barcaccia, designed by Pietro Bernini (p83)

▶ Stroll by Gian Lorenzo Bernini's 17th-century Fontana del Tritone (p77)

▰▰▰▰ Water played a central role in the development of Rome. The towering aqueducts, the thousands of *nasoni* (drinking fountains) and perhaps most famously the sculpted fountains that anchor the piazzas are testament to the city's intimate relationship with the element.

ROME BEST EXPERIENCES

← TREVI FOUNTAIN

Each year visitors throw €900,000 in coins into the Trevi Fountain. Whether or not your coin grants you a return to Rome, this spectacular baroque sculpture is well worth a visit.

→ **FONTANA DEI QUATTRO FIUMI**

One of Bernini's best-known works, the 1651 fountain in the middle of Piazza Navona is dedicated to the world's four major rivers known at the time: the Danube, the Nile, the Ganges and the Río de la Plata.

TOP WIRESTOCK CREATORS/SHUTTERSTOCK © BOTTOM CATARINA BELOVA/SHUTTERSTOCK ©

Above left Trevi Fountain
Left Fontana dei Quattro Fiumi

TRINKETS & TREASURES

There's no better way to experience Rome as a local than by visiting one of its many markets. Whether you're hunting for unique vintage items or you simply want to buy groceries to experiment with new recipes, the vibrant Esquilino, Porta Portese and Testaccio markets will welcome you with flavours, colours and sounds unseen elsewhere in the city. Looking for something more sophisticated? Head north for high-end stores.

Campo de' Fiori
Souvenirs and aperitivos
Built around a statue of Giordano Bruno, busy Campo de' Fiori is central Rome's best-known market. Long-time vendors now share the space with souvenir stalls, but bars and craft-beer pubs await in the back alleys.

from the Lungotevere or from Corso Vittorio Emanuele II ▶ p54

Porta Portese
Flea market
Rome's favourite Sunday market attracts more than 500 vendors selling books, secondhand clothing, vintage cinema posters, records and expensive antiques. Get here early and be ready to bargain as you dig for treasure.

to Via Portuense ▶ p130

Mercato di Testaccio
Street food
Open Monday to Saturday, the food market of the southern neighbourhood of Testaccio is one of the best places to experience Rome's culinary culture. You'll find freshly baked bread, *pizza rossa*, artisanal pasta and sweets, plus bars and cafes.

30 or 3 ▶ p155

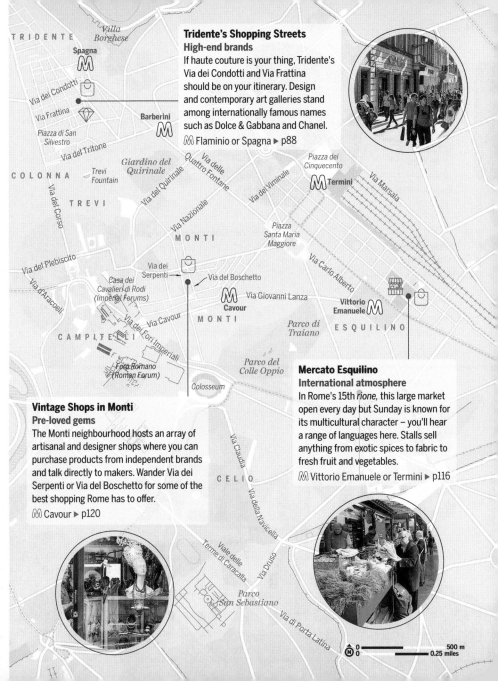

Tridente's Shopping Streets
High-end brands
If haute couture is your thing, Tridente's Via dei Condotti and Via Frattina should be on your itinerary. Design and contemporary art galleries stand among internationally famous names such as Dolce & Gabbana and Chanel.

Ⓜ Flaminio or Spagna ▸ p88

Vintage Shops in Monti
Pre-loved gems
The Monti neighbourhood hosts an array of artisanal and designer shops where you can purchase products from independent brands and talk directly to makers. Wander Via dei Serpenti or Via del Boschetto for some of the best shopping Rome has to offer.

Ⓜ Cavour ▸ p120

Mercato Esquilino
International atmosphere
In Rome's 15th *rione*, this large market open every day but Sunday is known for its multicultural character – you'll hear a range of languages here. Stalls sell anything from exotic spices to fabric to fresh fruit and vegetables.

Ⓜ Vittorio Emanuele or Termini ▸ p116

→ Visit the Domus Aurea

Escape the heat by stepping into the former residence of Emperor Nero, where the temperature hovers around 10°C year-round.

📍 Ancient Rome, p36

Lungo il Tevere Festival

Check out the Lungo il Tevere festival, held from June to August on the western bank of the Tevere river, with artisanal markets, shows and live music.

▶ lungoiltevereroma.it

Hear Some Jazz at Villa Celimontana

The Village Celimontana festival runs from June to September, with a rich program of jazz.

📍 San Giovanni, p147

▶ villagecelimontana.it

→ The Colosseum at Night

In July the 'Moon over the Colosseum' guided tours begin, taking you through an illuminated itinerary in the arena.

📍 Ancient Rome, p39

▶ parcocolosseo.it

JUNE

Average daytime max: 27°C
Average sun hours: 12.7

JULY

Rome in
SUMMER

↘ Gelato, Granita or Grattachecca?

Try gelato's refreshing cousins *granita al caffè* (crushed ice, sugar and espresso) at Tazza d'Oro and *grattachecca* (crushed ice with fruit syrup) at Sora Mirella's kiosk.

📍 Trastevere, p141

↓ Opera at the Baths of Caracalla

Rome's summer opera season takes place among the mesmerising ruins of the Baths of Caracalla – book tickets well in advance!

📍 Ancient Rome, p34

▶ operaroma.it

ROME PLAN BY SEASON

Swim at Nettuno

Take a day trip to the beach at Nettuno for a dip in the Tyrrhenian. It's just an hour away by train.

📍 Nettuno, p196

Average daytime max: 30°C
Average sun hours: 12.7

AUGUST

Average daytime max: 31°C
Average sun hours: 11.8

Isola del Cinema Film Festival

Head to the Isola Tiberina to watch a movie in the beautiful open-air setting of the Isola del Cinema film festival.

📍 Centro Storico, p61

▶ isoladelcinema.com

🧳 Packing notes
Sandals, shorts and sunscreen, plus a light scarf to cover your shoulders when entering churches.

Check out a full calendar of events

Boating at Villa Borghese

See the changing colours of central Rome's best-known park from a romantic lake setting.

📍 Northern Rome, p162

↘ Snack on Roasted Chestnuts

Street vendors selling *caldarroste* populate the city from October, adding to the vibrant street-food scene.

↘ Watch a Football Match

The Serie A champion-ship usually starts at the end of summer. Spend a Sunday cheering for Roma or Lazio (the city's two teams).

▶ legaseriea.it

Celebrity-spotting at the Film Festival

The Festa del Cinema di Roma takes place in October at the Auditorium Parco della Musica – go check out the red carpet!

📍 Northern Rome

▶ romacinemafest.it

SEPTEMBER

Average daytime max: 25°C
Average sun hours: 10

OCTOBER

Rome in
AUTUMN

↘ Follow the Sacconi Rossi procession

On 2 November the Sacconi Rossi friars hold a procession on the Isola Tiberina in memory of those who have drowned in the river.

📍 Centro Storico, p61

↓ Cycle the Appia Antica

Escape the city bustle by renting a bike and pedalling among the golden fields that surround the Appian Way.

📍 Southern Rome, p184

Walk Up to the Gianicolo

Sunset views hardly get better than those seen from the Gianicolo in the late-afternoon autumn light.

📍 Gianicolo, p136

ROME PLAN BY SEASON

NOVEMBER

Average daytime max: 21°C
Average sun hours: 8

Average daytime max: 16°C
Average sun hours: 6.5

October is high season (and autumn is often regarded as the best time to visit), so secure bookings well ahead.

🎒 Packing notes

The weather's still great: pack light, but don't forget a jacket as evenings can get chilly.

Shop & Eat at Christmas Markets

The most popular Christmas markets are in Piazza Navona, but many smaller squares also celebrate with brightly lit food and souvenir stalls.

📍 Centro Storico, p64

← Christmas Trees

Huge Christmas trees appear in Piazza Venezia, Piazza San Pietro (where you'll also find a nativity scene) and Piazza del Popolo.

↘ Light Installations

Shop for high-end brands under the magical installations of Via del Corso.

📍 Tridente

New Year at the Circo Massimo

Each year a large (and free) concert featuring international superstars is held at this former sporting stadium.

📍 Ancient Rome, p50

DECEMBER

Average daytime max: 12.5°C
Average sun hours: 6

JANUARY

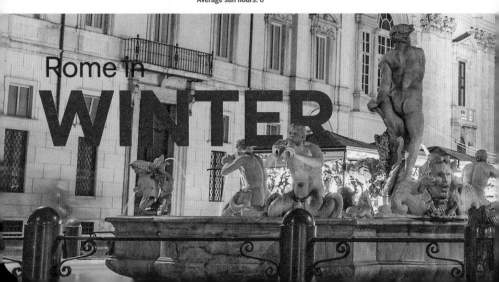

Rome in WINTER

⬎ Espresso at Caffè Sant'Eustachio

Often described as Rome's best espresso, the coffee served at Sant'Eustachio will give you the buzz you need to keep exploring.

📍 Centro Storico, p139
▶ santeustachioilcaffe.it

⬎ Museums Without the Crowds

The museums are less crowded in winter. Take your pick: modern art at the MAXXI or classical sculpture at the Capitoline Museums.

📍 Northern Rome, p171, or Ancient Rome, p40

Disappearing Rain in the Pantheon

Despite a 9m-wide oculus at the top of the Pantheon's dome, raindrops seem to disappear as they enter the structure.

📍 Centro Storico, p56

Orange-Tree-Garden Views

Walk up to Parco Savello for spectacular views of the city, surrounded by trees loaded with oranges.

📍 Aventino, p151

FEBRUARY

Average daytime max: 11.5°C
Average sun hours: 6

Average daytime max: 12°C
Average sun hours: 7

ROME PLAN BY SEASON

🎒 Packing notes
Bring comfortable closed shoes, a heavy sweater and a warm raincoat.

↘ Run (or Watch) a Marathon

Rome's marathon wends through the city centre's ancient ruins in March.

▶ runromethe marathon.com

Romics

Romics, in April, is one of Italy's most important international exhibitions on comics, animation and games.

▶ romics.it

↘ Stroll Through a Rose Garden

Walk in the Aventino's Roseto Comunale for the ultimate romantic experience: 1100 species of rose bloom in spring.

♥ Aventino, p151

↓ Visit the Botanical Gardens

Go for a walk in Rome's Orto Botanico to see the flora blooming as the days get longer.

♥ Trastevere, p134

MARCH

Average daytime max: 15°C
Average sun hours: 8

APRIL

Rome in
SPRING

↓ Concerto del Primo Maggio

The Labor Day Concert is Europe's largest free live-music event, hosting some of the best Italian acts in Piazza San Giovanni.

● San Giovanni

Picnic at Circo Massimo

The empire's sporting stadium is now a huge park that's perfect for a picnic as the weather gets warmer.

● Ancient Rome, p50

↘ Day-trip to Castel Gandolfo

Visit the Pope's summer residence and stroll the beautiful gardens surrounding the castle.

● Castel Gandolfo, p198

ROME PLAN BY SEASON

MAY

Average daytime max: 18°C
Average sun hours: 10

Average daytime max: 22.5°C
Average sun hours: 11

Packing notes

Prepare for moody weather: pack a light jacket, a scarf, comfy shoes and an umbrella.

MY PERFECT DAY IN
ROME

By Elisa Colarossi
@ @romangal
goesaround

STREET ART & OUT-OF-THE-WAY NEIGHBOURHOODS

▬▬▬▬ Rome is a wondrous open-air museum of art and history, and I've had the good luck to appreciate it all since I was a kid. But not everybody knows that the city is home to a wealth of contemporary art, especially on the street. Poster art, sticker art and graffiti bring the urban character of Rome to brilliant life, and its off-the-beaten-path neighbourhoods reflect it wonderfully. A colourful walk through Pigneto, Quadraro and Tor Pignattara is a must-do Roman expedition.

WHY I LOVE ROME
The light, the infinite shades of orange, the calm, the chaos. So many reasons to love Rome – but its poetry is the one for me.

Left Piramide di Caio Cestio **Right** Rome's streetside sticker art

ANCIENT RUINS, UNDERGROUND SECRETS & ROMAN FOOD

■■■■ Get off to a great start with thousand-year-old architecture at the Colosseum and the Forum. Carry on a stone's throw away at San Clemente Basilica to unearth layers of history and discover a beautiful Mithra temple. Book your Roman meal at Armando's near the Pantheon and head to Castel Sant'Angelo, crossing the scenic Ponte Sant'Angelo bridge. Spend your afternoon in Trastevere and visit the foundations of the Basilica di Santa Cecilia before heading to Seu Pizza Illuminati for a gourmet slice.

By Angela Corrias
@ @angela corrias

ANGELA CORRIAS/LONELY PLANET ©

↙ **BEST STOPS FOR FOODIES**

Otaleg (p133; pictured left) in Trastevere for classic gelato.

Supplizio (p73) near Campo de' Fiori for tasty street food.

Felice a Testaccio (p155) for *cacio e pepe* pasta.

ROME A DAY IN THE CITY

ARCHITECTURAL ODDITIES

By Angelo Zinna
@ @angelo_ zinna

■■■■ Walking south from the historical centre, you'll soon encounter the white-marble Piramide di Caio Cestio (12 BCE) by the busy roundabout encircling the 3rd-century Porta San Paolo. The mismatch gets better: steps away is the horseshoe-shaped Palazzo delle Poste (1935), made up of minimal straight lines and diagonal windows. Pass Blu's huge mural (2013) in Ostiense on your way to Garbatella, where the towering red Albergo Rosso (1929) exemplifies the *barocchetto romano* style that emerged during the neighbourhood's redevelopment in the 1920s.

WHY I LOVE ROME

Ruth Baettig's brass plate saying *Mi sono perso* (I am lost) hangs low on a wall near the Circo Massimo. It's a useful reminder: every time I get lost, Rome surprises me.

Things to Know About
ROME

INSIDER TIPS TO HIT THE GROUND RUNNING

1 Rioni, quartieri or municipi?

When looking at a map of Rome or an address, you might see different words for the city's neighbourhoods. The 22 *rioni* make up the historical centre, established in the Middle Ages. The 35 *quartieri* are the neighbourhoods surrounding the city core, outside the Aurelian Walls. The *rioni* and *quartieri* are contained within 15 *municipi* (administrative areas).

▶ For information about getting around Rome's neighbourhoods see p208

2 Cat City

It's no coincidence that many stray cats can be seen roaming the capital's streets: a 1991 Italian law states that cats have the right to occupy their colonies and should be protected from abuse. The Torre Argentina Feral Feline Colony is the oldest and largest in Rome, with a dedicated crew of volunteers tending to its pampered residents.

▶ Learn more about Rome's cats on p180

3 Football Devotion

Rome has two football teams playing in Serie A, Italy's top league. Lazio (blue and white) and Roma (red and gold) divide the city into two large groups of dedicated fans – don't mix them up!

4 Late Dinners

Italians usually have their evening meal after 8pm, so don't expect to be served before 7pm, especially outside the centre. Have an *aperitivo* instead! (The wonderful Italian tradition of *aperitivo* involves a buffet of snacks to accompany evening drinks, usually from around 6pm till 9pm.)

5 COVID-19

At the time of writing, COVID-19 regulations were still in place. To enter any enclosed public space – including public transport, shops and museums – you must wear a face mask. You may remove the mask when seated at a restaurant or drinking at a bar. To access restaurants, cinemas, theatres and museums you must also provide an EU Digital COVID Certificate (Green Pass) or proof of a negative COVID-19 test.

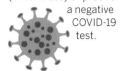

6 Roman Dialect

The Roman dialect, also known as Romanesco, is a language of its own, spoken only in the capital and surroundings. Fun and full of sarcasm, the local lingo has been popularised by national cinema and TV stars such as Alberto Sordi, Carlo Verdone and Gigi Proietti, becoming one of the most recognisable dialects among the many spoken in Italy.

Romans tend to drop the final syllable of verbs – for example, *andare* (to go) becomes *andà*. They also change prepositions by turning Ls into Rs – for instance, *del* (of) becomes *der*, and *nel* (in) becomes *ner*. There are also local terms and idioms not used elsewhere in Italy.

Here's your quick guide to the Romanesco lingo:

Bella Hi/bye (an alternative to *ciao*)

Daje! Come on!	**Avoja!** Of course!
Abbiocco Drowsiness	**Piotta** 100 euros
Bira Beer	**Na cifra** A lot
Nòne No	**Caciara** Hubbub
Pischello Kid	**Còre** Heart
Spaghi Spaghetti	**Ammazza!** Wow!
Mbé? So what?	**Se beccamo!** See you!

▶ Also see the Language chapter on p218

7 Two Countries in One

Your passport won't be stamped when you enter its museums, but since 1929 Vatican City has been an independent state. It's the smallest state in the world in terms of both size and population.

▶ Discover the Vatican Museums on p100

Read, Listen, Watch & Follow

 READ

The Street Kids
(Pier Paolo Pasolini, 1955) Originally censored, Pasolini's novel tells of children in Rome's poorer suburbs.

History: A Novel
(Elsa Morante, 1974) Follows the life of a single mother in fascist-era and WWII Rome.

The Secrets of Rome (Corrado Augias, 2007)
Rome's most controversial historical personalities.

Tentacles at My Throat
(Zerocalcare, 2012) The beloved comic artist on growing up in Rebibbia.

 LISTEN

Let's Do It Again
(Giuda, 2015) Roman glam rock: the band formerly known as Taxi brings British influences to the capital.

Coraggio (Carl Brave, 2020) The rap artist's second studio album features Italian pop and hip-hop greats.

This is Elodie
(Elodie, 2020) Pop, rap and R&B influences complement Elodie's powerful voice.

Cavallina (Adiel, 2019) One of Rome's best-known DJs creates hypnotic sounds that have led to international tours.

AWAKENING/GETTY IMAGES FOR CITY OF TURIN/GETTY IMAGES ©

Il Sorprendente Album d'Esordio de I Cani (I Cani, 2011; pictured above)
A pioneer of Rome's indie scene sings about growing up in the city.

▷ | **WATCH**

Bicycle Thieves (1948; pictured right) Vittorio de Sica's masterpiece depicts the harsh reality of postwar Rome.

Febbre da cavallo (1976) Comedy classic starring Gigi Proietti as an inept gambler.

Suburra: Blood on Rome (2017–20) Netflix crime series about mafia infiltration of Roman politics.

La grande bellezza (2013) Oscar-winning drama reveals the decadence of Rome's upper class.

Caro diario (1993; pictured right) Cult film about Vespa-riding director Nanni Moretti's relationship with his city.

LMPC/GETTY IMAGES ©

TCD/PROD.DB/ALAMY STOCK PHOTO ©

👤 | **FOLLOW**

Roma Culture
(@Sovrintendenza) Events, virtual tours and news.

parcocolosseo.it
Comprehensive info on Rome's archaeological area.

ansa.it/english
English-language Italian news.

Zero.eu
(@zero.eu) Events, up-and-coming artists and trends.

Romeing Magazine
(romeing.it) English-language news and travel tips.

ANCIENT ROME

ARCHAEOLOGY | ANCIENT HISTORY | RUINS

Experience
Ancient
Rome online

ANCIENT ROME
Trip Builder

TAKE YOUR PICK OF MUST-SEES AND HIDDEN GEMS

No matter how many times you've seen them in photographs, the monumental remains of Rome's ancient core are always a sight to behold. From the newly opened underground area of the Colosseum to the Forum's traces of pre-Christian beliefs, exploring the city's layered history yields endless surprises.

🗺 Neighbourhood Notes

Best for Ruins and historical architecture

Transport Take the metro to Colosseo or Circo Massimo, or a bus to Piazza Venezia.

Getting around Walking is the best way to explore the area.

Tip Ancient Rome gets crowded year-round, but with few after-dark attractions it's quieter at night.

Climb **Campidoglio** (p40), one of the seven hills on which Rome was founded, home of the Capitoline Museums.
🚶 *5 min walk from Piazza Venezia*

Via di San Marco

Discover the city's origins on the **Palatine Hill** (p44), the site of Rome's birth.
🚶 *2 min walk from the Colosseum*

Lgt Ripa

Tiber River

Parco Savello

Circo Massimo

Via de

Risk your hand in the **Bocca della Verità** (Mouth of Truth; p50), by the remains of ancient Rome's cattle market.
🚶 *10 min walk from Circo Massimo metro station*

Viale della Piramide Cestia

Via del Corso

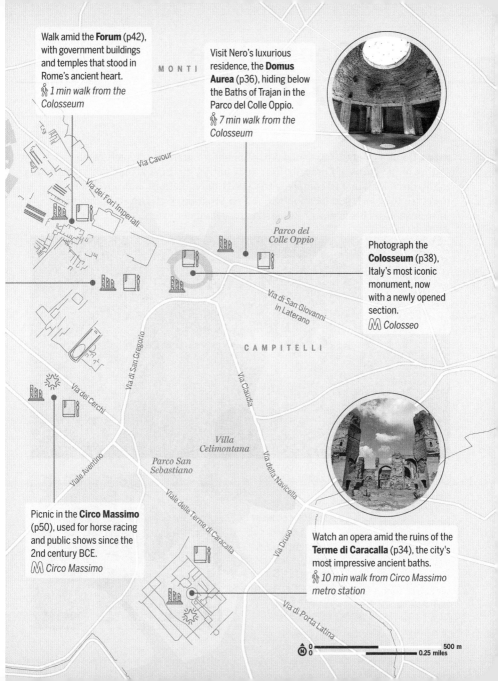

Walk amid the **Forum** (p42), with government buildings and temples that stood in Rome's ancient heart.

🚶 *1 min walk from the Colosseum*

MONTI

Visit Nero's luxurious residence, the **Domus Aurea** (p36), hiding below the Baths of Trajan in the Parco del Colle Oppio.

🚶 *7 min walk from the Colosseum*

Via Cavour

Via dei Fori Imperiali

Parco del Colle Oppio

Via di San Giovanni in Laterano

Photograph the **Colosseum** (p38), Italy's most iconic monument, now with a newly opened section.

Ⓜ *Colosseo*

CAMPITELLI

Via di San Gregorio

Via Claudia

Via dei Cerchi

Villa Celimontana

Via della Navicella

Parco San Sebastiano

Viale Aventino

Viale delle Terme di Caracalla

Via Druso

Picnic in the **Circo Massimo** (p50), used for horse racing and public shows since the 2nd century BCE.

Ⓜ *Circo Massimo*

Watch an opera amid the ruins of the **Terme di Caracalla** (p34), the city's most impressive ancient baths.

🚶 *10 min walk from Circo Massimo metro station*

Via di Porta Latina

ⓃⒹ 0 ——— 500 m
0 ——— 0.25 miles

01 Opera at the BATHS

MUSIC | THEATRE | ART

Rome's Opera House staged its summer program in the picturesque setting of the Baths of Caracalla from 1937 until 2019. In 2020 and 2021 it moved to the Circo Massimo to comply with COVID-19 regulations, but now it's ready to return to its original location with a rich program of classic and previously unseen shows. This is one of Rome's greatest summer events.

GLORIA IMBROGNO/SHUTTERSTOCK ©

📱 How to

Getting here Buses 118, 760 and 628 run to the Baths of Caracalla. The baths are five minutes on foot from Circo Massimo metro station.

Buying tickets Tickets can be purchased online via TicketOne or at the box office at Piazza Beniamino Gigli 1. Tickets cost between €25 and €110. Major shows sell out fairly quickly.

What's on? The full program is available at operaroma.it. Shows run for the whole of July and into August.

MAURO_REPOSSINI/GETTY IMAGES ©

DAVID IGNUT/SHUTTERSTOCK ©

Left Terme di Caracalla **Far left top** Max Gazzè performs at the Baths **Far left bottom** Teatro Costanzi

Music in the Baths One of antiquity's most important thermal complexes, built between 212 and 216 CE under the orders of Emperor Caracalla and once able to host 6000 to 8000 people per day, the setting of Rome's summer opera lives in the shadows of nearby attractions such as the Colosseum and the Forum, despite having maintained its imposing wall structures in excellent condition. Whether you're an opera fan or not, it's worth taking a couple of hours to step back in time here.

Big names For the past 80 years, Rome's summer opera has drawn audiences from all around the world, who come to immerse themselves in the majestic remains and evocative light show that form the backdrop to timeless masterpieces such as *The Barber of Seville* and *Notre-Dame de Paris*. Leonard Bernstein's *Mass: A Theatre Piece for Singers, Players and Dancers* is expected to open the 2022 edition, followed by three dates featuring shows by international dance superstar Roberto Bolle.

Not here in summer? Rome's Opera House runs shows year-round in its elegant Teatro Costanzi (Piazza Beniamino Gigli), not far from Termini station, and in the Teatro Nazionale (Via del Viminale 51). Reinterpretations of evergreen pieces such as Giuseppe Verdi's *Luisa Miller* and Giacomo Puccini's *Turandot* – whose 2022 scenography will be curated by Chinese artist Ai Weiwei – are highly anticipated.

The First Season at the Baths

The first opera season in the Baths of Caracalla was announced by Governor Don Piero Colonna in 1937 as part of a fascist-era project to bring theatre to the masses. Gaetano Donizetti's *Lucia of Lammermoor* launched the event in front of 7000 people on 1 August. The open-air opera began on the 2000th birthday of Rome's first emperor, Augustus, in a period in which Mussolini introduced cultural initiatives – such as the Augustan Exhibition of Romanity and the Exhibition of the Fascist Revolution – to celebrate an alleged continuity between the glorious imperial era and his totalitarian reign.

02 Nero's Forgotten
HOME

ARCHITECTURE | HIDDEN WONDER | WALL ART

▬▬▬ Undiscovered for centuries, Nero's Domus Aurea, erected after a fire destroyed Rome in 64 CE, was one of the most luxurious residences ever built, covering over 200 hectares. Nestled in the Parco del Colle Oppio, the Unesco-listed structure has yet to be fully excavated, but after a year of lockdown new sections have been uncovered and are ready to be explored.

UNDERWORLD/SHUTTERSTOCK ©

🗺 How to

Getting here Get off the metro at Colosseo and walk through the Colle Oppio park. You will find the entrance on your left.

Visiting The Domus Aurea is open 9am to 6.30pm daily. Visits are limited to the Sala Ottagona and surround-ings from Monday to Thursday (tickets €12), and extend to the whole structure from Friday to Sunday (tickets €18, including guide).

Bring a jacket The temperature inside the Domus Aurea is about 10°C year-round. Wear appropriate clothing.

ANTONY MCAULAY/SHUTTERSTOCK ©

Left Digital reproduction of the Domus Aurea in its heyday **Far left top** Domus Aurea interior **Far left bottom** Emperor Nero statue, Domus Aurea

ANCIENT ROME EXPERIENCES

Architecture Nero's luxurious residence was built in just over four years, under the supervision of architects Severus and Clever. The decorations were mostly painted by Fabullus, an eccentric artist known to always paint in his toga. The complex included massive pavilions and rooms for banquets, thermal baths and calming gardens, and over 150 rooms with vaulted ceilings that have remained intact under the Colle Oppio. At the heart of the structure was the Sala Ottagona, believed to have inspired the design of the Pantheon.

Erasing memory As one of the most hated emperors of Rome's history, Nero's legacy was quickly erased by his successors. Vespasian (69–79) began to destroy Nero's golden house and return the stolen building materials to the city by building the Colosseum. Titus (79–81) built his baths on the remains, and Trajan (98–177) built the grand thermal complex still visible today on the Colle Oppio, above the Domus Aurea.

New sections The year 2021 was significant for Roman archaeology. During the lockdown that emptied the city of tourists, efforts were made to uncover previously unseen sections of the Domus Aurea. Excavations have uncovered sculptures of the muse Talia, marble columns and fine capitals. An illuminated passageway designed by contemporary architect Stefano Boeri leading to the Sala Ottagona has been added to the itinerary.

Raphael's 'Grotesques'

Around 1480, Renaissance painters began descending into the Colle Oppio's foundations, hoping to find remnants of ancient Roman houses. Their torchlight explorations led to the discovery of frescoes believed to belong to the Baths of Titus. (The paintings actually belonged to the forgotten ruins of the Domus Aurea.) The frescoes were named 'grotesques' and became a key inspiration for Raphael, who repurposed the designs to decorate the Vatican Palace, making them hugely influential in the art world up to this day. The paintings in the Domus Aurea are still visible in many of the rooms.

03 Beneath the
ARENA

ARCHAEOLOGY | HISTORY | ARCHITECTURE

In June 2021, for the first time in history, the underground levels of the Anfiteatro Flavio – better known as the Colosseum – opened to the public. Discover an unseen section of Rome's best-known icon, and walk in the rooms where gladiators and animals prepared for spectacular fights in the arena, under the eyes of up to 50,000 blood-thirsty spectators.

🗺 How to

Getting here Access the Colosseum on its southern side along Via dei Fori Imperiali.

Best ticket deal Not all Colosseum tickets include access to the underground area. The best option is a Full Experience ticket (€22), which includes entry to the Forum and the Palatino.

Virtual guides The Y&Co app contains handy visual and audio guides in nine languages.

VIACHESLAV LOPATIN/SHUTTERSTOCK ©

Changing shapes The foundations of the Colosseum that are visible today were not built at the same time as the rest of the structure. Commissioned by Vespasian in 72 CE and completed by his son Titus in 80 CE, the stadium originally featured a wooden floor where trapdoors led to concealed rooms, cages and corridors where combatants and animals would prepare for the show. Domiziano (r 81–96) converted the subterranean levels into solid masonry, but their shape and structure continued to change for the following two centuries.

Above Colosseum **Right top** Detail of the Hypogeum **Right bottom** Colosseum interior

🎇 After Dark

From July to October the Colosseum's Archaeological Park organises hour-long guided evening tours where visitors can explore illuminated routes and immerse themselves in the enchanting atmosphere of the amphitheatre at night. Adult tickets start at €25. Check out parcocolosseo.it for booking options.

Preserved spaces While the upper part of the Colosseum continued to change after Valentinian III abolished gladiatorial games in 438, the underground spaces were buried in the 5th century and remained intact.

Hypogeum Below the Colosseum, 14 labyrinthine corridors radiate from the stadium. At the end of each narrow passage are the control rooms that housed the elevators used to transport animals, scenographic elements and people up to the sand-covered arena. After two years and 55,000 hours of restoration work, the hypogeum that served as the stadium's backstage (and was only partially visible until 2018) is now open to visitors via a new 160m-long walkway.

ANAME JIA18/GETTY IMAGES ©

ANAME JIA18/GETTY IMAGES ©

04 Public Art Across **THE AGES**

SCULPTURE | GALLERIES | HISTORY

▬▬▬ Sitting atop the Campidoglio, one of the seven hills on which Rome was founded, the Capitoline Museums were established in 1471, after Pope Sixtus IV donated a set of precious bronzes to the city. Open to the public since 1734, the museums offer insight into centuries of art-collection practices, capturing the evolving tastes and styles of rulers, popes and artists.

IOFOTO/SHUTTERSTOCK ©

🗺 **How to**

Getting here Piazza del Campidoglio is a 10-minute walk from Colosseo metro station and right behind Piazza Venezia, where several bus routes stop.

Tickets The museum is open 9.30am to 7.30pm daily. Purchase tickets (€11.50) via musei capitolini.org or at the ticket office in Palazzo dei Conservatori.

Two palaces The galleries are split between Palazzo dei Conservatori and Palazzo Nuovo.

ADAM EASTLAND/ALAMY STOCK PHOTO ©

Courtyard The 2.5m-tall head of Constantine the Great (280–337 CE) – belonging to the Colossus of Constantine found in the Basilica of Massenzio – welcomes you in the courtyard of Palazzo dei Conservatori, filled with marble fragments of millennia-old artworks.

Sala della Lupa The centrepiece of Palazzo dei Conservatori is the 5th-century-BCE bronze sculpture of the *Lupa Capitolina* (Capitoline Wolf). It's believed that the statue in its original form had little to do with Rome's foundation: the suckling Romulus and Remus, the city's founders of legend, were added only in the late 15th century.

Pinacoteca The 2nd floor of Palazzo dei Conservatori is home to a rich collection of paintings. Tracing the history of Italian fine art from 1350 to the 18th century, the eight rooms house masterpieces such as Rubens' *Romulus and Remus* (1612) and Guercino's *The Burial of St Petronilla* (1623), originally meant for St Peter's Basilica in the Vatican.

Sala dei Filosofi In Palazzo Nuovo, you can admire the statues of the *Dying Gaul* (230–220 BCE) and the *Capitoline Venus*. Steps away, the Philosophers' Room features a collection of marble busts of Roman and Greek philosophers (and writers). Stand among Homer, Socrates and Epicurus.

Above Constantine the Great statue relief **Far left top** *Lupa Capitolina* **Far left bottom** *The Burial of St Petronilla*, Pinacoteca Capitolina

☀ Piazza & Palazzo to Peruse

Before you dive into the museum's treasures, take a moment to admire the elliptical Piazza del Campidoglio, designed in 1538 by Michelangelo. Between the museum's two palaces is the Palazzo Senatorio, one of the world's oldest municipal buildings, hosting the city hall since 1144.

05 Walk the
VIA SACRA

TRIUMPHAL ARCHES | TEMPLES | RUINS

Once the most important road of the Roman Forum Valley, the Via Sacra cut through ancient Rome's beating heart, connecting the Regia (the residence of the kings) with the Capitoline Hill. Monumental memorials, religious structures and political buildings line the 2000-year-old basalt-slab thoroughfare used to celebrate Roman triumphs.

PITYCZECH/GETTY IMAGES ©

🗺 Trip Notes

Tickets You can buy single-day (€16) or two-day (€22) tickets at parcocolosseo.it. They're each valid for one visit to the Forum.

Listen up Downloadable audio guides are available for €3.99 on the Parco Colosseo app.

Views Walk up to Piazza del Campidoglio or the Palatine Hill for incredible views.

Stay hydrated There are few shaded areas in the Forum. If you are visiting in summer, be sure to bring water.

🏛 Casa delle Vestali

The House of the Vestal Virgins (pictured above), a temple dedicated to Vesta, the virgin goddess of family and home, is near the remains of the Regia as you enter the Via Sacra. Vestal Virgins, girls aged between six and 10, lived in the temple to maintain the sacred fire.

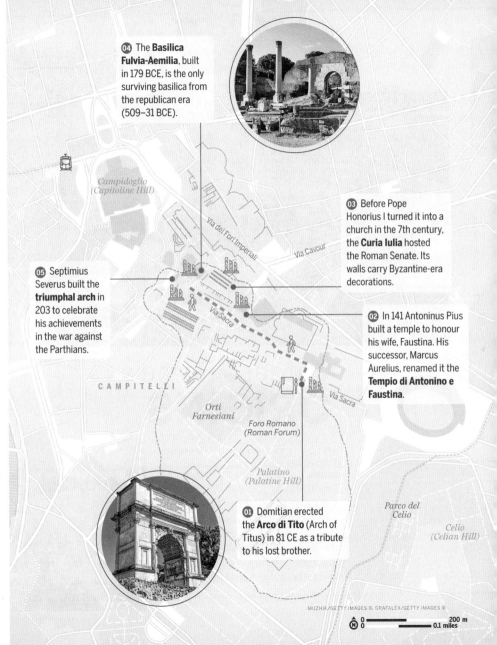

04 The **Basilica Fulvia-Aemilia**, built in 179 BCE, is the only surviving basilica from the republican era (509–31 BCE).

Campidoglio (Capitoline Hill)

03 Before Pope Honorius I turned it into a church in the 7th century, the **Curia Iulia** hosted the Roman Senate. Its walls carry Byzantine-era decorations.

Via dei Fori Imperiali

Via Cavour

05 Septimius Severus built the **triumphal arch** in 203 to celebrate his achievements in the war against the Parthians.

Via Sacra

02 In 141 Antoninus Pius built a temple to honour his wife, Faustina. His successor, Marcus Aurelius, renamed it the **Tempio di Antonino e Faustina**.

CAMPITELLI

Orti Farnesiani

Foro Romano (Roman Forum)

Via Sacra

Palatino (Palatine Hill)

Parco del Celio

Celio (Celian Hill)

01 Domitian erected the **Arco di Tito** (Arch of Titus) in 81 CE as a tribute to his lost brother.

MUZHIK/GETTY IMAGES ©, GRAFALEX/GETTY IMAGES ®

N 0 | 200 m
   0 | 0.1 miles

06 Witness Rome's
ORIGINS

HISTORY | ARCHAEOLOGY | RUINS

Rome's oldest nucleus is found among the lush greenery of the Palatine Hill. With traces of human activity dating back to the Iron Age, the area nestled between the Roman Forum and the Circo Massimo is believed to be the site where Romulus founded the city.

🗺 How to

Getting here Get off the metro at Colosseo and walk to the entrance at Via Gregorio 30.

Tickets Single-day (€16) or two-day Full Experience (€22) tickets are available via parcocolosseo.it.

Palatine Museum Sculptures, fresco fragments and remains retrieved by archaeologists in over two centuries of excavation can be seen here. Entry is included in the Full Experience ticket.

Romulus & Remus

Legend tells that Vestal Virgin Rhea Silva, daughter of Numitor, the king of Alba Longa, became the mother of twin boys Romulus and Remus after she was raped by Mars. Her brother Amulius, fearing that the throne would pass to one of the newborns, ordered the boys' murder. The soldiers charged with the deed chose to spare the infants and abandoned them in a basket on the River Tiber. A she-wolf living in the Palatine Hill spotted the crying boys on the riverbank and brought them to her lair, where she fed them until they were found by a farmer. Growing up, the brothers decided to build a city, but a disagreement about its location led Romulus to kill Remus and found Rome on the Palatine Hill in the middle of the 8th century BCE.

📖 She-Wolf or Woman?

The legend of the Lupa, the she-wolf that saved Romulus and Remus, has endured down the centuries, but the wolf may actually have been a woman. In Latin, *lupae* meant prostitute (ancient Rome's brothels were known as *lupanari*). The city icon could be due to a misinterpretation.

Left Orti Farnesiani (Farnese Gardens) **Above left** Circo Massimo **Above right** She-wolf statue, Ponte Flaminio

Casa Romuli

The dwelling where it's said Romulus grew up was identified in 1946 in the southwestern corner of the Palatine. Archaeologists found the remains of a group of small huts containing organic materials dating back to the early Iron Age, a period in line with Rome's origin story. Looking at the barely visible traces of this ancient settlement, it's difficult to conceive of Rome's vast expansion in the following millennia.

Opulent Residences

The luxurious Palace of Domitian, built during the emperor's reign in the late 1st century CE, was an enormous structure designed to flaunt the seemingly endless power and resources of Rome's ruler. Rediscovered in the 18th century, the palace is divided into three sections: the Domus Augustana, the Domus Flavia and the stadium. The Domus Augustana, built on two levels by architect Rabirus, was the private residence of the emperors, with rooms leading

🌿 Europe's Oldest Botanical Garden

Cardinal Alessandro Farnese established the Horti Palatini Farnesiorum in 1537 to collect previously unseen plants arriving from the Americas. Agave, yucca and Peruvian passiflora were planted among baroque statues in a network of terraces and water courses. By the early 17th century the Farnese family had purchased almost the entire surface of the Palatine Hill. The magical Orti Farnesiani is considered to be the oldest botanical garden in Europe.

Left Casa Romuli Far left Orti Farnesiani Below Domus Flavia

to porticoed courtyards surrounding a large fountain whose remains are still visible today.

The Domus Flavia was the space for public meetings. Extending from the Aula Regia, the rectangular room where the emperor would meet his most important guests, it includes a basilica where the ruler could deal with legal matters and a large peristyle surrounding a pool with an octagonal marble island emerging from its centre.

The Stadium

Measuring 160m long and surrounded by a two-storey portico, the semicircular *stadio* built by Domitian appears as soon as you enter the Palatine Hill. Rediscovered in the 18th century, the stadium hosted private games for the enjoyment of rulers. For a great view of the stadium and the archaeological area, walk to the Arcate Severiane, a double set of brick arches built to expand the surface of the Palatine Hill by creating an artificial plane where an extension of the Flavian Palace was meant to be erected.

ANGELO ZINNA/LONELY PLANET ©

Bitter Symbols

FACING UP TO ROME'S FASCIST PAST

As the world turns its attention to the impact of monuments dedicated to oppressive historical figures, Italy confronts the residue of its darkest decades. How to deal with the traces of Benito Mussolini's totalitarian regime?

In Rome you never have to look far to find remnants of the *ventennio* – the era between 1922 and 1943 when Mussolini ruled the country. If you arrive at Termini, Italy's largest railway station, rebuilt to Angiolo Mazzoni's 1939 plan, you'll be greeted by 225,000 sq metres of classical forms clad in Italian white marble, then an imposing atrium intended to convey the city's imperial character.

Fascist-era architects employed vast spaces, monumentalism and design emulating Rome's ancient structures to evoke austerity, nationalism and continuity with the past. At the Foro Italico sports complex, a 17.5m obelisk carrying the engraving MVSSOLINI DVX still stands. The EUR district, built for Rome's 1942 Universal Exhibition, features the Palazzo della Civiltà Italiana (also known as the Square Colosseum) and the Museum of Roman Civilization.

Much of the regime's imposing architecture was repurposed after WWII. The building that housed the Ministry of Italian Africa, near the Circo Massimo, now hosts the headquarters of the Food and Agriculture Organization (FAO), and in 2021 the archives of Mussolini's former Colonial Museum were reopened for the first time in 40 years in an attempt to recontextualise the relationship between Italy and the African territories it colonised – a history of violence long repressed in public discourse, which will be represented in the new Museo Italo Africano 'Ilaria Alpi'.

But it's often the subtler symbols that pack the biggest punch. Streets such as Viale Eritrea, Via Somalia, Viale Libia and Viale Etiopia are reminders of Italy's efforts to subjugate African peoples. Beginning in the 19th century, these endeavours reached their peak in the 1930s when Italy declared itself an empire.

Left Foro Italico **Middle** Obelisco di Mussolini, Foro Italico **Right** Palazzo della Civiltà Italiana

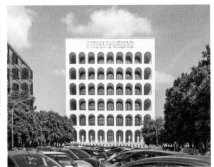

An increasing number of authors and artists have committed to exposing the flaws in the country's collective memory and deconstructing the myth of the 'good Italian'. Italo-Somali writer Igiaba Scego, author of *Adua* and one of the most prominent voices on the topic, believes that attitudes can only change through education and an accurate retelling of history. The cultural landscape seems to be moving in this direction.

> Fascist-era architects employed vast spaces, monumentalism and design emulating Rome's ancient structures to evoke austerity and continuity with the past.

Valerio Ciriaci's 2015 documentary *If Only I Were That Warrior*, about the Eritrean occupation of 1935, was a response to the installation of a monument to fascist general Rodolfo Graziani in Affile, just outside Rome.

Following the wave of international statue-toppling protests that began after the death of George Floyd at the hands of US police in May 2020, activists have sought to reframe the meaning of some of Rome's urban landmarks. In mid-June 2020 a bust of General Antonio Baldissera, an engineer of Italian colonialism in Eritrea, was covered in pink paint. On the same day, the sign for Via Amba Aradam – named after the mountainous area of Ethiopia where, in 1936, Marshal Pietro Badoglio's troops defeated the Ethiopian army using illegal poison-gas weapons – was papered over to change the street's name to Via George Floyd e Bilal Ben Messaud. In May 2020 Messaud, a migrant from Tunisia, drowned off the coast of Sicily while 'fleeing forced confinement on a ship', according to anti-racist activists.

Reading Rome's Recent History

History: A Novel, by **Elsa Morante (1974)** Ida Ramundo, a Jewish teacher living in the San Lorenzo district, finds herself alone and raising her children, Nino and Useppe, during WWII.

Adua, by Igiaba Scego **(2015)** Adua came to Rome during the Somali diaspora of the '70s. In an attempt to make sense of her identity, she tells Bernini's famous 'Elefantino' statue the story of her father, Zoppe, who worked as an interpreter during the fascist regime.

The Woman of Rome, by **Alberto Moravia (1947)** Adriana recounts the relationships she enters during the fascist years, in a story of greed, corruption and moral decline.

Listings

BEST OF THE REST

More Ancient Monuments

Arco di Costantino

Right behind the Colosseum, the 21m-high triumphal Arch of Constantine was erected in 315 CE to celebrate the emperor's victory against Maxentius.

Bocca della Verità

Hung on the wall of the church of Santa Maria in Cosmedin since 1632, the marble sculpture known as the Bocca della Verità (Mouth of Truth) will bite your hand off if you lie to it. Allegedly.

Trajan's Markets

Built in the early 2nd century under Trajan's rule by architect Apollodorus of Damascus, Trajan's Markets were the Forum's administrative centre. Today, they can be visited as part of the Museum of the Imperial Fora.

Circo Massimo

Nestled between the Aventine and Palatine Hills, the Circo Massimo was the largest entertainment venue of antiquity, covering approximately 85,000 sq metres. Now it's a park used for concerts and sporting events – you can picnic among the ruins.

🏛 Galleries & Museums

Palazzo Venezia

The infamous palace where Mussolini had his office. Today, the palace houses the National Museum of Palazzo Venezia and the headquarters of the National Institute of Archaeology and Art History.

Rhinoceros Gallery

Opened in 2018, Rhinoceros is a modern art gallery near the Foro Boario (cattle market)

managed by the Alda Fendi Foundation. The Palazzo Rhinoceros was designed and furnished by Pritzker Prize–winning architect Jean Nouvel.

Ala Brasini al Vittoriano

The Ala Brasini section of Piazza Venezia's Vittoriano building, also known as the Altar of the Fatherland, brings rotating exhibits of contemporary work to Piazza Venezia. Recent shows have featured Jackson Pollock, Andy Warhol and Fernando Botero.

Galleria Colonna

Steps from the church of Santi Apostoli, the Galleria Colonna is a lesser-known gem housing the Renaissance art collection that belonged to the Colonna family in the 17th and 18th centuries.

Bites Between Sights

Osteria Circo   €€

Local dishes prepared with prime-quality ingredients and served in a warm, rustic and welcoming setting that features dark-wood surfaces and neutral tones. Try the *bucatini all'amatriciana* – you won't regret it.

Arco di Costantino

SEAN XU/SHUTTERSTOCK ©

Zerosettantacinque €€

The lively Zerosettantacinque (0.75) by the Circo Massimo has it all: friendly staff, refined comfort food inspired by both local and international traditions, and a huge selection of alcoholic and non-alcoholic drinks.

Perpetual €€€

Refined yet informal, fine-dining joint Perpetual offers a health-conscious menu designed by chefs Cezar Predescu and Paolo Cappuccio in the restaurant's lab. For dessert, be sure to leave some space for the hazelnut sablè with coconut ganache.

Crab €€€

Flavours of the sea are on offer at Via Capo d'Africa 2. From raw-fish dishes to oysters, Crab serves a continuously changing menu of fresh seafood in a modern, light-filled space that's three minutes from the Colosseum.

🍷 Tasty Drinks & Spectacular Views

The Court €€€

The rooftop bar of Palazzo Manfredi in Via Labicana offers splendid views of the Colosseum. Stop by for an experimental cocktail or two in the heart of ancient Rome.

Terrazza Caffarelli €

The panoramic cafeteria on the top floor of the Capitoline Museums is one of the best spots to enjoy a coffee or daytime drink while admiring the city ruins from above.

Terrazza Caffarelli

Race Club €€

Open daily until 3am, the unassuming Race Club at Via Labicana 52 is your go-to bar for late-night sips, a cosy, old-school atmosphere, and surprising concoctions crafted by experienced bartenders.

Coming out €€

With over 20 years of history, gay bar Coming Out is an institution. Open daily from 8am to 2am, the venue serves breakfast, lunch, dinner and late-night drinks right by the Colosseum.

Caffè Propaganda €€

At Via Claudia 15, the sophisticated Caffè Propaganda is an ideal stop for a well-deserved break between sights. There's a vast selection of tea, wines and spirits, plus cheese and cured-meat boards to go with your *aperitivo*.

Scan for more things to do in Ancient Rome

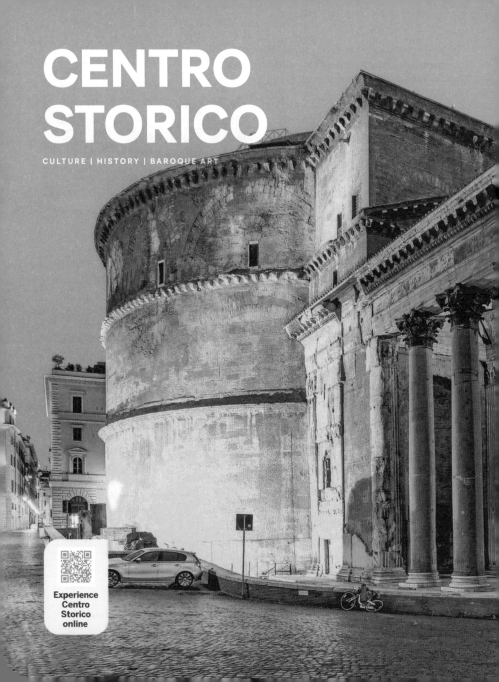

CENTRO STORICO

CULTURE | HISTORY | BAROQUE ART

Experience
Centro
Storico
online

CENTRO STORICO
Trip Builder

**TAKE YOUR PICK OF MUST-SEES
AND HIDDEN GEMS**

Rome's Centro Storico covers a small fraction of the city's area, but with treasure-filled baroque churches and palaces, lively piazzas and dozens of cobblestone alleys that extend from the neighbourhood's main artery, Corso Vittorio Emanuele II, you could spend weeks exploring the rich heritage of Rome's beating heart.

🗺 Neighbourhood Notes

Best for Opulent palaces, art galleries and piazza-hopping

Transport Walk from Barberini metro station or take a bus to Petroselli or Torre Argentina.

Getting around All attractions can be reached on foot.

Tip Locals avoid restaurants in the main squares. Choose backstreet eateries such as La Montecarlo, MyAle or Barnum.

Giardini di Castel Sant'Angelo

Lgt Castello

Tiber River

Lgt Tor di Nona

Ponte Principe Amedeo

PONTE

Walk across **Piazza Navona** (p64), built atop a stadium among monumental fountains and baroque *palazzos*.
🚶 *5 min walk from Torre Argentina*

PARIONE

Lgt Gianicolense

Lgt D Sangallo

Stroll through **Campo de' Fiori**, central Rome's best-known market, surrounding a monument to heretic Giordano Bruno.
🚶 *6 min walk from Torre Argentina*

Tiber River

Lgt Raphaello Sanzio

Via Benedetta

Gianicolo (Janiculum Hill)

Via Garibaldi

GIANICOLO

0   500 m
0   0.25 miles

Admire three Caravaggios dedicated to St Matthew in the **Chiesa di San Luigi dei Francesi** (p63) – for free.

🚶 *3 min walk from the Pantheon*

Step into the **Pantheon** (p56), one of ancient Rome's best-preserved buildings, originally a pagan temple.

🚶 *15 min walk from Barberini metro station*

Gaze at Andrea Pozzo's *Gloria di Sant'Ignazio* trompe l'oeil fresco in the **Chiesa di Sant' Ignazio di Loyola**.

🚶 *6 min walk from the Trevi Fountain*

Marvel at the **Galleria Doria Pamphilj** (p63), one of Rome's richest private art collections, with works by Renaissance masters.

🚶 *5 min walk from Piazza Venezia*

Sink your teeth into a fried artichoke in one of the famed Judeo-Roman restaurants of the **Jewish Ghetto** (p66).

🚶 *5 min walk from Torre Argentina*

Discover the healing practices and rituals of the **Isola Tiberina** (p60), one of the world's smallest inhabited islands.

🚶 *5 min walk from Petroselli bus stop*

Map labels:

Via Tomacelli
COLONNA
Via del Corso
Via delle Quattro Fontane
Giardino del Quirinale
TREVI
Via Zanardelli
Corso del Rinascimento
SANT'EUSTACHIO
PIGNA
CENTRO STORICO
Corso Vittorio Emanuele II
Via del Plebiscito
Via Panisperna
Via delle Botteghe Oscure
Via d'Aracoeli
REGOLA
Via Arenula
SANT'ANGELO
Jewish Ghetto
Campidoglio (Capitoline Hill)
Lgt D Sangalio
Lgt de Cenci
Foro Romano (Roman Forum)
CAMPITELLI
Ponte Garibaldi
Isola Tiberina
Lgt dei Pierleoni
Via Petroselli
Via Renella
Ponte Palatino
Via del Circo Massimo
Via dei Cerchi
Tiber River
Lgt Ripa
Parco Savello

07 Contemplating the **PANTHEON**

RELIGION | ARCHITECTURE | HISTORY

Once a pagan temple dedicated to the seven planetary deities, the Pantheon is Rome's best-preserved ancient building, an engineering feat whose design has been hugely influential throughout its 2000-year history. Behind 16 Corinthian columns and two 12m-tall bronze doors hides the monumental concrete dome with its oculus (eye) – a 9m-wide opening meant to allow contemplation of the skies.

PAOLO GALLO/SHUTTERSTOCK ©

🗺 **How to**

Visiting The Pantheon is open 9am to 7pm. Access is free, but visitor numbers are restricted. Expect long lines.

Celebrations Catholic rituals have been held in the Pantheon since 609. Mass takes place at 5pm on Saturdays and 10.30am on Sundays.

Royal tombs In 1878 the Pantheon was chosen as the final resting place for Italy's royalty. The remains of Vittorio Emanuele II and Umberto I are buried here, next to the tomb of Renaissance artist Raphael.

FB STUDIO/SHUTTERSTOCK ©

Layered history Erected in 27 BCE, the Pantheon has changed shape multiple times. The inscription on the lintel at the entrance says: 'Built by Marcus Agrippa, son of Lucius, in the year of his third consulship', but the Pantheon's current form was conceived by Hadrian, who ordered its reconstruction in 112 CE after the former structure burned down. In 609 the temple was converted into a church, taking the name it carries to this day: Basilica di Santa Maria ad Martyres.

Stolen goods In August 1625 Pope Urban VIII, a member of the Barberini family, removed the bronze joints of the Pantheon's porch beams and used them to build cannons for Castel Sant'Angelo and Bernini's baldachin at St Peter's Basilica. This gave rise to the saying, 'What the barbarians didn't do, the Barberini did'. Fortunately, the elegant polychrome marble that covers the floor and most of the internal walls is still original.

The dome Apart from the missing bronze, the Pantheon's awe-inspiring architecture has remained for the most part intact. The dome's beautiful ceiling coffers aren't just decorative: the sunken panels help reduce the roof's weight. To avoid the massive structure from collapsing onto itself, the Pantheon's architects had to use increasingly lighter materials as they approached the oculus. With a diameter of 43.4m, the dome was the world's largest until the 15th century.

Above left Tomb of Vittorio Emanuele II **Far left top** Dome interior **Far left bottom** Pantheon facade

 Rain in the Dome

It's often said that when it rains, water somehow doesn't enter the Pantheon's oculus. Of course, this is not true – at least, not entirely. Rain does indeed enter the open dome, but thanks to an updraft that forms on the inside, raindrops are broken down into tiny droplets that are almost invisible to the naked eye. The 'chimney effect' transforms water into mist, which disappears shortly after it touches the ground thanks to a convex floor and a barely visible drainage system.

08 Palazzo Spada
ILLUSIONS

ARCHITECTURE | SCIENCE | ART

Hiding in the Secret Garden of the 16th-century Palazzo Spada is an optical illusion created by architect Francesco Borromini in 1653. Thanks to a design technique known as forced perspective, you'll struggle to believe that the 37m-long column-lined gallery leading to the courtyard is, in fact, shorter than 9m.

MARCOVARRO/SHUTTERSTOCK ©

How to

Getting here Palazzo Spada is located in Piazza Capodiferro, steps from Palazzo Farnese, one of the city's most prestigious High Renaissance palaces.

Visiting You can't walk through Borromini's gallery any more, but volunteers working at the museum often informally demonstrate the optical illusion to visitors.

Entry fee It costs €5 to visit the museum and Borromini's gallery.

The art of illusion In 1413 Florentine artist Filippo Brunelleschi developed a mathematical system to depict three dimensions on canvas, initiating the scientific study of perspective. It wasn't long before architects began experimenting with geometry to build deceptive structures meant to leave spectators dumbfounded.

Palazzo Spada In 1632 Cardinal Spada purchased a 1540 palace to turn into a luxurious residence for his family and his vast art collection. To refurbish the palace, he hired the eccentric

Above Borromini's gallery **Right top** *The Botanist*, Bartolomeo Passerotti **Right bottom** Palazzo Spada interior

🖼 Palazzo Paintings

The four rooms of the museum feature an impressive collection of baroque paintings, with works such as Passerotti's *The Botanist* and Tornioli's *The Astronomers*.

Borromini, who was making a name for himself as the city's leading architect.

Forced perspective Borromini's gallery was inspired by the cardinal's key moral warning: material greatness is nothing more than an illusion. A series of architectural devices contribute to the optical effect. The white marble Doric columns appear to be all the same height, but in fact they steadily decrease in size: the closest pair is 5.8m tall and the furthest away only 2.45m. The sloping floor and ceiling are tiled with a pattern of shrinking squares, and the seemingly life-size statue of Mars, standing at the end of the gallery, is only 60cm tall.

The result is an astonishing work that puzzles the eye – an artifice of baroque art that fools viewers, making it seem that this courtyard in the heart of the city occupies a space much larger than its actual area.

09 Rituals of Isola
TIBERINA

HISTORY | ESOTERICISM | MYTHOLOGY

Connected to Trastevere and the Jewish Ghetto by the Cestio (44 BCE) and Fabricio (62 BCE) bridges, the ship-shaped Isola Tiberina floats in the River Tiber, carrying traces of ancient beliefs, esoteric ceremonies and miraculous healing rituals. It's one of the world's smallest inhabited islands.

🗺️ How to

All Souls' Day On 2 November a torchlight procession runs from the Chiesa di San Bartolomeo to the Fatebenefratelli hospital.

Carbonara stop? Sora Lella (Via di Ponte Quattro Capi 16) has been operating since 1959.

Oldest Roman stone bridge From the island's southern tip there's a clear view of the 2nd-century-BCE Pons Aemilius, better known as Ponte Rotto (Broken Bridge).

God of Medicine In 293 BCE Rome was in the grip of a plague, so a delegation went to Greece to ask Asclepius, the God of Medicine, for help. A snake (Asclepius' symbol) climbed onto the delegates' ship and, as the ship returned to Rome, plunged into the Tiber and swam to the Isola Tiberina. In 291 BCE Rome recovered from the plague and the Senate built a temple to Asclepius on the site of the snake's disappearance.

Temple remains A staircase by the Ponte Cestio takes you down to the riverbank. Beyond the island's tip you'll find some travertine blocks shaped like a ship's prow – these belonged to the Temple of Asclepius, in use until the 4th century CE. The relief of a snake embracing Asclepius' rod, now an international symbol of medicine, is still identifiable.

Chiesa di San Bartolomeo San Bartolomeo (1000 CE) stands in the temple's location. Next to the altar, a medieval well gave access to water believed to have miraculous properties.

Sacconi Rossi In the 18th century the church was occupied by the Sacconi Rossi (Red Cloaks) friars, who retrieved the unclaimed corpses of those who had drowned in the Tiber and placed them in a crypt. Contact I Viaggi di Adriano (pigierre. com) or Romolo e Remo for a permit to visit the crypt.

Far left top Ponte Cestio and the Isola Tiberina Far left bottom Chiesa di San Bartolomeo interior

🎬 Isola del Cinema

Running from mid-June to September in conjunction with the riverside Lungo il Tevere festival, the Isola Tiberina sets the stage for a season of outdoor, open-air cinema, showcasing the best new Italian and international films, some shown in their original language. There are also meetings and Q&A sessions with actors, writers and directors, masterclasses and other film-related events.

10 Caravaggio
DREAMING

ART | CULTURE | PAINTING

███████ Around 1592 Michelangelo Merisi, better known as Caravaggio, moved to Rome to work for the nobility. Despite his famously troubled character – which led to a death sentence for the murder of Ranuccio Tommasoni in 1606 – during his Roman years Caravaggio refined the theatrical use of light and composition that would make him one of the most influential artists of all time.

LEEMAGE/CORBIS VIA GETTY IMAGES ©

🗺 Trip Notes

Free art While entering private galleries will set you back between €10 and €14, access to all churches is free.

Holy beer For a break between chapel and gallery, stop at La Botticella pub in Via di Tor Millina. Run by the welcoming Giovanni, La Botticella is one of the few pubs to sell Tre Fontane beer, produced on the outskirts of Rome at one of the world's 14 Trappist abbeys.

✓ More Caravaggio

Beyond this itinerary, you can see *Judith Beheading Holofernes* (pictured above) in Palazzo Barberini, *The Entombment of Christ* in the Vatican Museums, and *The Conversion of St Paul* and *The Crucifixion of St Peter* in the Basilica di Santa Maria del Popolo. The Galleria Borghese has the largest collection of Caravaggio's works.

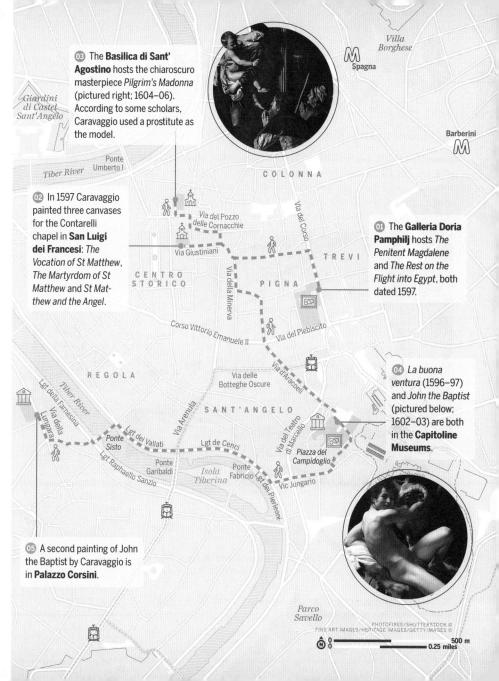

03 The **Basilica di Sant' Agostino** hosts the chiaroscuro masterpiece *Pilgrim's Madonna* (pictured right; 1604–06). According to some scholars, Caravaggio used a prostitute as the model.

02 In 1597 Caravaggio painted three canvases for the Contarelli chapel in **San Luigi dei Francesi**: *The Vocation of St Matthew*, *The Martyrdom of St Matthew* and *St Matthew and the Angel*.

01 The **Galleria Doria Pamphilj** hosts *The Penitent Magdalene* and *The Rest on the Flight into Egypt*, both dated 1597.

04 *La buona ventura* (1596–97) and *John the Baptist* (pictured below; 1602–03) are both in the **Capitoline Museums**.

05 A second painting of John the Baptist by Caravaggio is in **Palazzo Corsini**.

Villa Borghese

Spagna

Barberini

Giardini di Castel Sant'Angelo

Tiber River

Ponte Umberto I

COLONNA

Via del Pozzo delle Cornacchie

Via del Corso

Via Giustiniani

CENTRO STORICO

Via della Minerva

TREVI

PIGNA

Corso Vittorio Emanuele II

Via del Plebiscito

REGOLA

Tiber River

Lgt della Farnesina

Via della Lungara

Via delle Botteghe Oscure

Via d'Aracoeli

SANT'ANGELO

Lgt dei Vallati

Via Arenula

Lgt de Cenci

Via del Teatro di Marcello

Piazza del Campidoglio

Ponte Sisto

Ponte Garibaldi

Lgt Raphaello Sanzio

Isola Tiberina

Ponte Fabricio

Lgt dei Pierleoni

Vic Jungario

Parco Savello

N   0   500 m
     0   0.25 miles

11 Revelatory Piazza
NAVONA

LANDMARKS | PUBLIC ART | MONUMENTAL SCULPTURES

Built on the remains of the Unesco-listed Stadio di Domiziano, horseshoe-shaped Piazza Navona has some of Rome's most fascinating monumental fountains and baroque palaces. But not all art is standing in plain sight: classical masterpieces, inimitable antiques, mysterious symbols of power and even a 'talking statue' await in the backstreets.

GIVAGA/GETTY IMAGES ©

🗺 Trip Notes

When to go The piazza's Chiesa di Sant'Agnese in Agone and the Fontana dei Quattro Fiumi get busy. Arrive early to avoid crowds.

Hydration Rome's monumental fountains pour drinkable water, but it's best to use any of the 2000 *nasoni* (drinking fountains) installed throughout the city to fill your bottle.

Views The Terrazza Borromini Restaurant, on the top floor of Palazzo Pamphilj, offers the best views of Piazza Navona.

🏛 Stadio di Domiziano

Once a 30,000-seat arena, the 265m-long stadium built by Domiziano between 85 and 86 CE is still partly visible under Piazza Navona. The archaeological museum that houses the remains of the stadium sits 4.5m below the square and is accessible through Via di Tor Sanguigna. Entry is €8.50.

Giardini di
Castel
Sant'Angelo

Ponte
Umberto I

Tiber River

04 In Piazza San
Apollinare, the
elegant 15th-century
Palazzo Altemps
holds a fine collection
of ancient sculpture.

Via G Zanardelli

05 In **Via dei Coronari**, Galleria
dei Coronari sells treasures
from the past, while Creart
produces ceramics inspired by
the Roman tradition.

03 At **Sant'Ivo alla
Sapienza** bees are
everywhere: the
Barberini coat of arms
is sculpted into the
walls of the church,
completed by
Borromini in 1660.

PONTE

Via dei Coronari

01 Bernini's **Fontana dei Quattro
Fiumi** (1651) is the most impressive
of the square's three fountains,
though Fontana del Moro (pictured
left) and Fontana del Nettuno are
also awe-inspiring.

Via Santa Maria
dell'Anima

Piazza
Navona

Corso del Rinascimento

PARIONE

CENTRO
STORICO

SANT'EUSTACHIO

02 The **Pasquino statue** is
one of the 'talking statues' that
once dotted the city. Citizens
hung anonymous signs around
its neck to display complaints.

N
0   200 m
0   0.1 miles

12 Tasting the GHETTO

FOOD | JEWISH HERITAGE | CULTURE

The Jewish Ghetto has much more than artichokes *alla giuda* to offer those in search of a meal: stuffed zucchini flowers, *aliciotti* (anchovies), fish broth, cod in batter and potato meatloaf are all part of a culinary tradition that dates back centuries.

How to

Getting there The Jewish Ghetto is accessible via the beautiful remains of the **Portico d'Ottavia**, an ancient walkway built in 131 BCE that connects to the Teatro Marcello.

Book ahead Judeo-Roman cuisine is popular with both locals and tourists. Reserve a table in advance, especially if you're in a group.

Costs A two-course meal in the Ghetto will cost you upwards of €25.

CENTRO STORICO EXPERIENCES

A Brief History of the Ghetto

There's been a Jewish community in Rome since the 2nd century BCE: in 161 BCE the Jews of Palestine asked Rome for protection against the attacks of Hellenistic king Antiochus IV Epiphanes in Judea and Samaria. In less than a century Rome's Jewish population grew to 40,000 people. Ostracism, however, also increased as governments changed: under Constantine (r 306–37 CE) Jews were prohibited to hold public office or serve in the military. In 1215 Pope Innocent III forced Jews to wear a yellow or blue mark in public in order to be identifiable. In 1555 Pope Paul IV introduced a law that forced the Jewish community to live in a walled quarter whose two gates were locked at night. The Ghetto was born. The Jewish community continued to experience waves of hatred, violence and

Turtle Fountain

Legend has it that the late-16th-century **Fontana delle Tartarughe**, in the Piazza Mattei, was built overnight by Duke Mattei to prove his power to his future father-in-law, who lived in one of the palaces overlooking the square. Attributed to Bernini, the bronze turtles were added a century later.

Left Fried young artichokes **Above left** Alfresco dining, the Ghetto **Above right** Wall-mounted Jewish symbols, the Ghetto

discrimination until the end of the fascist era in the late 1940s.

Milk or Meat?

Centuries of isolation and strict adherence to *kashrut* (Jewish religious laws around food) have contributed to a unique culinary heritage that's worth sinking your teeth into. The signature dish of Judeo-Roman cuisine is the *carciofo alla giuda* (fried artichoke), found in every restaurant on Via Porto d'Ottavia and surroundings. But apart from a few shared vegetarian delicacies, menus vary widely. *Kashrut* rigidly prohibits the consumption of meat and milk together, so restaurants serve one or the other.

Yotvata (Piazza Cenci 70), for instance, is a milk restaurant, serving kosher cheese boards next to a plate of *concia* (marinated and fried zucchini). **Bellacarne** (Via del Portico d'Ottavia 51), as the name suggests, prepares certified meats in a variety of ways, from kosher carbonara to tomahawk steaks

Keeping Memory Alive

'A person is only forgotten when their name is forgotten', says the Talmud. Inspired by this, German artist Gunter Demnig installed a series of golden *stolpersteine* (stumbling stones) in Via della Reginella bearing the names of those who perished during the Nazi-fascist persecution. Passers-by stumble and see the names, and the memory of the victims endures.

To learn more about the history of Rome's Jewish community, visit the **Jewish Museum** in the Great Synagogue (Tempio Maggiore di Roma; 1904). Seven galleries trace the story of the Ghetto through a collection of 1500 objects and documents.

Left Via della Reginella **Below** Jewish pastries

to codfish fillets. Ba'Ghetto, which claims to be the oldest Jewish restaurant in Rome, has solved the problem of milk-meat contamination by opening three restaurants on Via Porto d'Ottavia: **Ba'Ghetto**, **Ba'Ghetto Milky** and **Su'Ghetto**, specialising in kosher Italian dishes.

Time for Dessert

When it comes to sweets, **Boccione** (Via del Portico d'Ottavia 1) is a Roman institution. Run by the same family for over two and a half centuries, Boccione bakes classic almond-cinnamon cookies, *trecce* (braided pastries) with candied fruit, and Roman breakfast favourites such as croissants and fried *bombe* (doughnuts). Its speciality, however, is the mouth-watering *torta ricotta e visciole* – a cake filled with sweet ricotta and sour cherries that has been made to the same recipe for 50 years.

ROME'S ANIMALS,
Wild & Imagined

01 La Lupa

The legendary she-wolf that saved the city's twin founders Romulus and Remus is Rome's best-known icon.

02 Papal Bees

Bees, representing hard work, were the symbol of the Barberini family, to which Pope Urban VIII belonged, and decorate churches such as Sant'Ivo alla Sapienza.

03 Parrocchetti

Imported as pets from the tropics and released by negligent owners, green parrots have reproduced in the thousands.

04 L'Aquila

Symbol of Jupiter – king of the gods – the eagle has represented power since the imperial era.

05 L'Elefantino

Odd and beloved, Bernini's Elefantino statue stands under a 6th-century-BCE Egyptian obelisk in Piazza della Minerva.

06 Turtles

Marking the centre of the Jewish Ghetto, the Fontana delle Tartarughe features four realistic turtles attributed to Bernini.

07 Asclepius' Snake

Adopted internationally as the symbol of med- icine, the rod of Greek god Asclepius appears in the remains of the Temple of Asclepius on the Isola Tiberina.

08 Deer of St Eustace

High on the front of Sant'Eustachio Basilica is a deer with a cross between its antlers – a tribute to the sacred animal that led to the saint's conversion.

09 Horses

From the winged horses of the Trevi Fountain to the rampant horses of the Dioscuri Fountain and the Equestrian Statue of Marcus Aurelius in the Capito- line Museums, equines are all around the city.

10 Cats of Torre Argentina

In Rome's historical centre a colony houses dozens of felines that roam among ancient ruins.

Listings

BEST OF THE REST

Interesting Bars & Iconic Enotecas

Open Baladin   €€

With 40 beers on tap and 100 bottles from the best Italian brewers, the Open Baladin pub near Campo de' Fiori is a must-stop for any craft-beer enthusiast. Try the Garden smoked beer or the Zucca pumpkin ale.

MyAle   €€

Nestled in Via dei Cappellari, a quiet Campo de' Fiori backstreet, MyAle offers a wide selection of craft brews alongside delicious focaccia filled with local ingredients including cured meats and artisanal cheeses. Closed Sunday.

Jerry Thomas Speakeasy   €€

Listed five times in the World's 50 Best Bars, the Prohibition-era-inspired cocktail bar named after New York bartender Jerry P Thomas will take you back to the roaring '20s – but only if you know the password.

Bar del Fico   €€

Stop by this historical cocktail lounge in the heart of the city for an *aperitivo* or two. Its elegant atmosphere has made it popular among hip locals.

L'Angolo Divino   €€€

L'Angolo Divino, run by welcoming sommelier Massimo Crippa, has an impressive cellar filled with hundreds of carefully selected bottles. Ask Massimo for a natural-wine recommendation – you won't be disappointed.

Il Piccolo   €€

Relaxed spot on the busy Via del Governo Vecchio, steps from Piazza Navona. The knowledgeable staff of this small *enoteca* serves plenty of intriguing labels by the glass, accompanied by pastas, bruschettas and salads.

Il Goccetto   €€

With nearly 40 years of history behind it, Il Goccetto is loved by locals, who are often found sipping wine on the street under the Vino Olio sign. Its cold plates make the perfect *aperitivo*.

Pizza, Pasta or a Quick Bite?

Antica Friggitoria La Masardona   €

If Roman pizza isn't your thing, head to La Masardona, by the Tiber. Go for a takeaway Neapolitan-style *pizza fritta* or stay for a soft, oven-baked margherita topped with *fior di latte* mozzarella, buffalo mozzarella and *provola* cheese.

Mimì e Cocò   €€

The warm atmosphere and friendly staff at Mimì e Cocò make for a safe choice in Via del Governo Vecchio. High-quality Roman fare at reasonable prices. If you're staying for dessert, be sure to try the tiramisu.

Open Baladin

La Montecarlo   €

Fast, loud and busy, La Montecarlo is a no-frills restaurant that has served thin, crispy Roman pizza since the late 1980s.

La Ciambella   €€

Farm-to-table cooking creates contemporary interpretations of popular classics, all served in an elegantly curated location with a calming neutral palette. Bookings recommended.

Barnum   €

Vegetarian-friendly lunch spot serving light plates and great coffee in a chilled atmosphere. You could easily come here to work in the morning (free wi-fi) and stay until night.

Antico Forno Roscioli   €

The Antico Forno Roscioli doesn't need an introduction: it's been making excellent bread and pizza since 1972. Given its fame, prices have gone up in recent years, but a slice of its *pizza rossa* is still worth paying for.

Supplizio   €

Supplì are a staple of Roman street food. You never have to walk far to find deep-fried rice balls filled with tomato sauce and mozzarella, but chef Arcangelo Dandini has reinvented the *friggitoria* experience, offering a rich menu of fried foods that pay tribute to tradition while offering surprising flavour combinations.

Forno Campo de Fiori   €

One of the few eateries in Campo de' Fiori to stay true to its roots. Forno Campo de' Fiori's white pizza with mortadella has a loyal fanbase that won't be convinced to go elsewhere – no matter the crowds.

Quinto Gelateria   €

Opened shortly after the end of WWII, Quinto stands out among the tourist traps near Piazza Navona, offering homemade ice cream in changing flavours and generous smoothies made from fresh fruit.

Gelato, Piazza Navona

📖 Books & Crafts

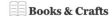

Altroquando

New and secondhand books, with a great graphic-novel section. The culture doesn't stop at words – underneath the bookshop is a hidden pub selling craft beers and cocktails.

ONEROOM

Specialising in photography books, ONEROOM is a treasure trove for visual-arts enthusiasts.

Creart

Handmade decorative ceramics paying tribute to nature, architecture and religion and inspired by designs of the past.

L'Image

The friendly staff of L'Image will help you navigate the colourful collection of paper and canvas prints, original posters and postcards.

Co.Ro.Jewels

Jewellery inspired by architecture, hand-crafted in the heart of Rome, from industrial bracelets to wearable pagodas.

Scan for more things to do in Centro Storico

CENTRO STORICO REVIEWS

TRIDENTE, TREVI & THE QUIRINALE

ART | ARCHITECTURE | SHOPPING

Experience
Tridente,
Trevi & the
Quirinale
online

TRIDENTE, TREVI & THE QUIRINALE
Trip Builder

TAKE YOUR PICK OF MUST-SEES AND HIDDEN GEMS

▬▬▬▬ Home to monumental squares and elegant *palazzi,* this area boasts art galleries, baroque architecture and exciting places to eat. Don't miss highlights such as the Spanish Steps and the Trevi Fountain, but be sure to enjoy a traditional meal and some artisanal gelato, too.

🗺 Neighbourhood Notes

Best for History, grand palaces and trendy shopping streets

Transport Take the metro to Flaminio, Spagna or Barberini.

Getting around Especially in summer, buses can be packed. Avoid peak hour, and walk or take the metro instead.

Tip Seek out hidden gems in the backstreets.

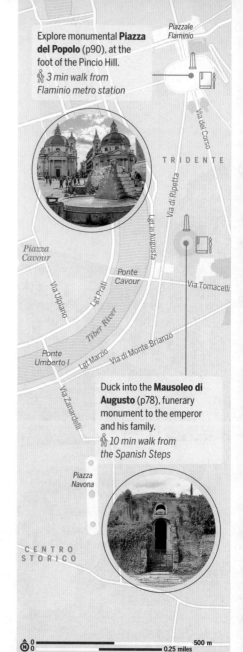

Explore monumental **Piazza del Popolo** (p90), at the foot of the Pincio Hill.
🚶 *3 min walk from Flaminio metro station*

Piazzale Flaminio

Via del Corso

TRIDENTE

Via di Ripetta

Lgt in Augusta

Piazza Cavour

Ponte Cavour

Via Tomacelli

Via Ulpiano

Lgt Prati

Tiber River

Ponte Umberto I

Lgt Marzio

Via di Monte Brianzo

Via Zanardelli

Duck into the **Mausoleo di Augusto** (p78), funerary monument to the emperor and his family.
🚶 *10 min walk from the Spanish Steps*

Piazza Navona

CENTRO STORICO

🇳 0 — 500 m
0 — 0.25 miles

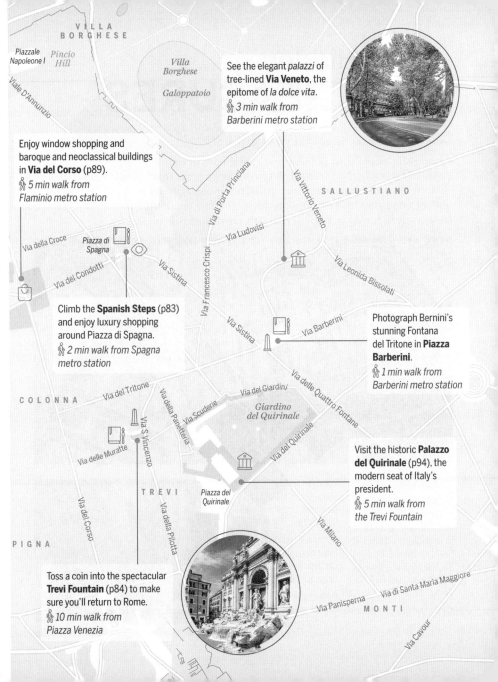

VILLA BORGHESE

Piazzale Napoleone I

Pincio Hill

Viale D'Annunzio

Villa Borghese

Galoppatoio

See the elegant *palazzi* of tree-lined **Via Veneto**, the epitome of *la dolce vita*.
🚶 *3 min walk from Barberini metro station*

Enjoy window shopping and baroque and neoclassical buildings in **Via del Corso** (p89).
🚶 *5 min walk from Flaminio metro station*

Via di Porta Pinciana

Via Vittorio Veneto

SALLUSTIANO

Via della Croce

Piazza di Spagna

Via del Condotti

Via Sistina

Via Francesco Crispi

Via Ludovisi

Via Leonida Bissolati

Climb the **Spanish Steps** (p83) and enjoy luxury shopping around Piazza di Spagna.
🚶 *2 min walk from Spagna metro station*

Via Sistina

Via Barberini

Photograph Bernini's stunning Fontana del Tritone in **Piazza Barberini**.
🚶 *1 min walk from Barberini metro station*

COLONNA

Via del Tritone

Via della Panetteria

Via Scuderie

Via del Giardini

Via delle Quattro Fontane

Giardino del Quirinale

Via del Quirinale

Via delle Muratte

Via S Vincenzo

TREVI

Piazza del Quirinale

Visit the historic **Palazzo del Quirinale** (p94), the modern seat of Italy's president.
🚶 *5 min walk from the Trevi Fountain*

Via del Corso

Via della Pilotta

Via Milano

PIGNA

Toss a coin into the spectacular **Trevi Fountain** (p84) to make sure you'll return to Rome.
🚶 *10 min walk from Piazza Venezia*

Via Panisperna

Via di Santa Maria Maggiore

MONTI

Via Cavour

13

Hidden
TREASURES

ARCHAEOLOGY | ARCHITECTURE | CHRISTIANITY

▬▬▬▬ Some of the most popular neighbourhoods in central Rome, Tridente, Barberini and Trevi have hidden gems that visitors will love to unearth. From little-known passageways to underground sites, these places provide a welcome break from the crowds lining up in front of the city's most famous landmarks.

VIVIDA PHOTO PC/SHUTTERSTOCK ©

STEFANO MONTESI/CORBIS VIA GETTY IMAGES ©

🗺 How to

Getting here Reach the Mausoleo di Augusto by bus (119, 628) or metro to Flaminio; the Capuchin Crypt by bus (52, 63, 80, 83, 160, 590) or metro to Barberini; and Galleria Sciarra by bus (62, 119, 160, 492).

When to go The Mausoleo di Augusto and Capuchin Crypt are open 9am to 7pm.

Costs Admission to the Mausoleo di Augusto is €4, to the Capuchin Crypt €8.50.

Bookings Mandatory for the Mausoleo di Augusto (mausoleodiaugusto.it).

VILLA BORGHESE

Flaminio M
Piazza del Popolo
Galoppatoio
Villa Medici
Via del Babuino
TRIDENTE
Spagna M
Via Vittorio Veneto
Via Boncompagni
Mausoleo di Augusto
Tiber River
Via dei Condotti
Via del Corso
Via dei Due Macelli
Via Sistina
Via del Tritone
Chiesa di Santa Maria della Concezione
M Barberini
COLONNA
TREVI
Via del Quirinale
M Repubblica
Via Marco Minghetti
Palazzo Sciarra Colonna
Galleria Sciarra
Piazza dell'Oratorio
N
0   500 m
0   0.25 miles

Ancient Rome Reopened after 14 years of renovation, the Mausoleo di Augusto has been restored to its original splendour. It's the largest round burial chamber of the ancient world, 87m across and 45m high. Start your tour by crossing the long corridor, passing three niches containing urns. Around the central building area is a series of ring-shaped concentric corridors.

Go underground The 17th-century Chiesa di Santa Maria della Concezione, built by Pope Urban VIII Barberini, is in Via Veneto. Despite the church's artwork, which includes such paintings as *San Michele Arcangelo* by Guido Reni, visitors tend to remember the eerie Capuchin Crypt, decorated with the bones of at least 4000 friars who died between 1528 and 1870. Cross the thin corridor to other chambers, where you will see mummified monks wearing their robes, and skeletons including Princess Barberini, holding a scythe in her right hand and a scale in her left.

Secret passageway Galleria Sciarra is a Liberty-style jewel of central Rome. In the wake of Italian unification, when Rome was due to become the new capital, many buildings underwent full renovation, including the complex of Palazzo Sciarra Colonna. The passageway connecting Via Minghetti to Piazza dell'Oratorio was painted by Giuseppe Cellini between 1885 and 1888. Its main theme is a celebration of women's virtues and roles from motherhood to loyalty.

Far left top Galleria Sciarra **Far left bottom** Mausoleo di Augusto interior

🏛 Augustus & His Mausoleum

Built in 28 CE after his victory over Mark Antony and Cleopatra in Actium, the Mausoleo di Augusto was the final resting place Augustus envisioned for himself and his family. Used as a funerary mausoleum for more than a century, the monument went into a state of disrepair when succeeding emperors began to build their own tombs. In its heyday the monument almost reached the height of nearby Pincio Hill. It was built near the river to be visible from most parts of the city.

Baroque
BARBERINI

ART | HISTORY | ARCHITECTURE

██████ You'll hardly find a part of Rome that isn't steeped in history, and Palazzo Barberini is no exception. An outstanding example of the Italian baroque, it was built by leading 17th-century architects Carlo Maderno and rivalry-stricken duo Gian Lorenzo Bernini and Francesco Borromini. Part of the Galleria Nazionale d'Arte Antica, the museum displays works dating from the 13th to 18th centuries.

MARCOVARRO/SHUTTERSTOCK ©

🗺 **How to**

Getting here The *palazzo* is near Via Veneto. Get here by metro (Barberini, line A) or bus (62, 63, 81, 160, 492).

When to go Palazzo Barberini is open 10am to 6pm Tuesday to Sunday; it's closed 25 December and 1 January.

How much Entry is €10 for adults; reductions apply (see barberini corsini.org).

Top sight It's hard to miss Pietro da Cortona's giant fresco decorating the ceiling of the entrance hall.

T.KKURINAWA/GETTY IMAGES ©

ROBERTO SERRA · IGUANA PRESS/GETTY IMAGES ©

Above left Borromini's helicoidal staircase **Far left top** Pietro da Cortona's ceiling fresco **Far left bottom** Palazzo Barberini

History Wander the *palazzo's* corridors picturing the former owners in their imposing mansion. Maffeo Barberini, head of the powerful clan (and who would later become Pope Urban VIII), acquired the villa from the Sforza family and commissioned Carlo Maderno to design a new building. Instead of demolishing the existing villa, Maderno ambitiously connected it to a parallel wing through a central strip, giving the palace an innovative H-shape.

Masterpieces Tucked away among larger canvases is a tiny portrait of a young woman. Until not long ago this was believed to be the portrait of Roman patrician Beatrice Cenci on the eve of her beheading in 1599 – thousands came to see the painting on the basis of this story. Nearby is Caravaggio's gory *Giuditta e Oloferne* (Judith Beheading Holophernes), and although historians disagree, it's hard to dispel the story that says the artist painted it after witnessing Cenci's execution.

Illustrious rivalry The eternal one-upmanship between Bernini and Borromini fed much 17th-century Roman gossip and animated literary and historical debate. Before they competed over high-profile commissions within the Vatican palaces and around the city, Bernini and Borromini worked side by side in Palazzo Barberini. Today visitors can drink in their legacy, from Borromini's mesmerising helicoidal staircase to Bernini's sculptural portrait of Pope Urban VIII.

🏛 Thirst for Power

Originating in Tuscany, the Barberini family amassed huge wealth through farming. All they were missing was a noble rank – until the son of Antonio da Barberino became Pope Urban VIII in 1623.

During the 21 years of his reign, the Papal State and the city of Rome underwent a period of great artistic development, land reclamation, agricultural boosts and political reform. All this entailed unpopular decisions that the pope deemed necessary to finance his ambitious plans, from imposing new taxes to decorating his mansion with ancient Roman relics.

15

Above & Beyond
THE STEPS

ART | RELIGION | HISTORY

 Chiesa di Trinità dei Monti dominates the view over the Spanish Steps, yet it's hardly visited – and it's a pity. Commissioned by French king Louis XII and consecrated in 1585, the church complex includes a cloister, intriguing examples of perspective anamorphic works, and beautiful frescoes. Climb the famous steps to discover this lesser-known landmark.

🗺 How to

Getting here Take the metro to Spagna.

When to go The church is open daily year-round. English tours of the church and cloister are held on the second and fourth Wednesdays of the month from mid-September to July.

Tickets Tours are €12; bookings (trinitadeimonti. net) are mandatory.

Tip To avoid stairs, use the Spagna metro station lift.

ACKAB PHOTOGRAPHY/SHUTTERSTOCK ©

Church Built roughly on the site of the palace of the 1st-century Horti Luculliani on the slopes of Pincio Hill, Chiesa di Trinità dei Monti offers great views over Rome from its front staircase.

Inside, cross the single-nave interior and stop at each of the six side chapels to see Daniele da Volterra's painting *Deposizione* (Deposition; c 1546) and the works of other 16th-century artists such as Perin del Vaga and Giulio Romano.

Cloister The cloister is a treasure trove of art. Admire the *Mater Admirabilis* fresco of a praying holy Mary that

Above Chiesa di Trinità dei Monti **Right top** *Deposizione*, Daniele da Volterra **Right bottom** Spanish Steps

📖 Keats-Shelley House

The Keats-Shelley Memorial House (ksh.roma.it), where English poet John Keats died in 1821, displays a collection of his books and personal objects, along with those of his fellow Romantics Lord Byron and Percy Bysshe Shelley. Nearby, you can enjoy an English-style tea experience at Babington's Tea Rooms.

young novice Pauline Perdreau painted in a corridor, then move towards the anamorphoses to experience the optical illusions that priests Emmanuel Maignan and Jean-François Niceron created. Complete your tour at the astrolabe on the 1st floor, where Maignan's scientific calculations of the sun's rays mark the time and the positions of stars and planets.

Spanish Steps A cornerstone of Italian baroque, the steps (all 136 of them) were built in the 18th century. Pope Urban VIII commissioned the Barcaccia fountain, at the base of the steps, from Pietro Bernini, who completed it in 1629 with the help of his more famous son, Gian Lorenzo.

16 Trevi Fountain
FOLKLORE

ART | ARCHAEOLOGY | AQUEDUCTS

In-the-know travellers will appreciate looking at one of Rome's most striking landmarks, the Trevi Fountain – location of a famous scene from Fellini's film *La Dolce Vita* – from an unusual perspective. Go underground and follow local traditions to explore a charming quarter steeped in history.

SVETLANASF/SHUTTERSTOCK ©

📍 How to

Getting here Take the metro to Barberini, or bus 100 or 119.

When to go The sites are open all year. For a quieter experience, avoid summer and Christmas time.

How much Admission to the Aqua Virgo ruins is €4. Bookings are mandatory; call 06 06 08.

Gelato stop Take a break at historic Il Gelato di San Crispino.

History The ancestor of Rome's most scenic fountain was built in the 1st century BCE by Roman politician Agrippa to connect the Aqua Virgo aqueduct to Rome to feed his thermal baths. Somewhere around the 8th century the aqueduct was halted, and this minor spring became its last fountain. The site underwent centuries of renovation, with the occasional intervention of stars such as Bernini. Roman artist Nicola Salvi was commissioned to complete the final project of the monumental masterpiece we see today.

Above Statue of Oceanus **Right top** Detail of Triton and horse **Right bottom** Trevi Fountain at night

✅ Ruins & Multimedia

In the lower levels of La Rinascente department store in Via del Tritone you can view the arches of the ancient Aqua Virgo aqueduct and a multimedia presentation about other nearby ruins currently not visible.

From beneath Some 300m from the fountain you can visit the Aqua Virgo underground archaeological site. Head to Via del Nazareno to see three minor arches and a bigger fornix identified as the arch built by emperor Claudius. An inscription commemorates Claudius' renovation of the Aqua Virgo in 46 CE.

Lovers' token The fountain has accrued various folk traditions. The most famous one tells visitors that if they throw a coin over their shoulder into the water, they will certainly come back to Rome. Local couples have for a long time sealed their love beside the small nearby spring, known as the lovers' fountain, by drinking its water from the same, never-used-before glass and then breaking it.

JOLANTA WOJCICKA/SHUTTERSTOCK ©

BLUE PLANET STUDIO/SHUTTERSTOCK ©

SANDRIXROMA/SHUTTERSTOCK ©

Roman Empire Aqueducts

UNDERSTANDING ANCIENT ROME'S SOPHISTICATED PIPING SYSTEM

Alongside roads and thermal baths, aqueducts are the most well-known and spectacular infrastructure dating to ancient Roman times. Demonstrating the importance of water in Roman civilisation, these impressive feats of engineering can be seen in many cities and regions of the former empire.

Left Parco degli Acquedotti **Middle** Nero's Aqueduct **Right** Aqua Claudia, Porta Maggiore

Even though it's widely known as the Eternal City, Rome has another, very revealing moniker: Regina aquarium (Queen of Water). Water played a crucial role in many aspects of Roman social, private and political life. 'The importance of water in ancient times is linked to its wide use', explains Marta Baumgartner, archaeologist at Soprintendenza Speciale di Roma, the heritage authority of the Ministry of Culture. 'Alongside its daily public service, water was needed to supply the big thermal baths built throughout the centuries by emperors, as well as for the villas with *horti* (big gardens) and the *domus* (wealthy houses) that often featured ornamental fountains.'

For centuries the River Tiber and local wells were enough to supply the needs of the territory, but as Rome expanded and its population began to increase, a more efficient system of pipes became necessary. Therefore, from around the 4th century BCE skilful builders and engineers made it their goal to create a wide network of aqueducts. Still the subject of study, these sophisticated examples of public engineering provided Rome with a vast amount of drinking water – more than in any other city in the ancient world.

A spring needed particular features, including the quality, flow and level of its water, to become the source of a successful aqueduct. Everything was carefully planned, including the filtering process and an advanced mechanism that determined whether the waterway was going to run in the open air or through an underground tunnel.

There were 11 main aqueducts in ancient Rome. Their huge archways were needed to overcome uneven terrain and ensure the necessary downward slope. The first of

the waterways, according to 'aqueduct curator' Frontinus in 97 CE, was the Aqua Appia, built in 312 BCE by censor Appius Claudius Caecus (who is also known for the Appian Way, one of ancient Rome's most famous roads). The first two waterways, Aqua Appia and Anio Vetus, run almost entirely underground; the others, including the Aqua Marcia, Aqua Traiana and Aqua Claudia, feature majestic arches and vaults.

> These sophisticated examples of public engineering provided Rome with a vast amount of drinking water – more than in any other city in the ancient world.

From the Aqua Claudia, Emperor Nero built a branch to supply water ornaments and fountains in his magnificent Domus Aurea palace, while different pipes from Aqua Marcia supplied an array of neighbourhoods, including the Quirinale, Capitoline Hill, Celio and Aventine Hill, as well as the Baths of Caracalla, thanks to a separate pipeline built by Emperor Caracalla.

Wandering the streets of Rome, travellers will come across the ruins of several ancient aqueducts. The final part of the Anio Vetus can be seen in the Esquilino; in Porta Maggiore there are the overlapping Aquae Claudia, Marcia, Tepula, Iulia and Anio Novus; and if you take a walk in Via Aurelia you will see Aqua Traiana. In Via Domenico Fontana, near San Giovanni in Laterano Basilica, visitors can see remnants of Nero's aqueduct, and the point where the Aquae Marcia, Tepula and Iulia join is visible at Porta Tiburtina.

🏛 Discover Parco degli Acquedotti

At Parco degli Acquedotti, southeast of Rome, you can see the 16th-century Aqua Felice, built by Pope Sixtus V Felice Peretti atop the Aquae Claudia and Marcia.

Nearby Parco di Tor Fiscale is worth a visit because the Aqua Marcia and the Aqua Claudia cross paths in two places. The medieval Torre del Fiscale is built on top of one of these intersections. In the other, the archways form a polygon known as the barbaric camp: the Ostrogoths settled here when they besieged Rome.

Recommended by Marta Baumgartner, *archaeologist at Soprintendenza Speciale di Roma, the supervising authority for heritage for the Ministry of Culture.*

17 Rome's Shopping STREETS

FASHION | ART | SHOPPING

Clothes, shoes, accessories, artisan homewares: you say Italy, you say luxury shopping. Whether you're looking for the best gifts to take home or something to remember your trip by, throughout Rome's Tridente district you'll be spoilt for choice.

🗺 Trip Notes

Getting here Take the metro to Flaminio for Piazza del Popolo and Tridente or a bus (40, 64, 70, 81, 492, 628) to Piazza Venezia and Via del Corso.

When to go Wait until January for the winter sales or July for the summer discount season.

Quick lunch Stop at Ginger (Via Borgognona 43) for a healthy, tasty meal indoors or alfresco.

🏛 Via Margutta

Historic little Via Margutta (pictured above) is a longtime favourite with artists and celebrities. Italian director Federico Fellini lived at No 110 with his wife, actress Giulietta Masina.

Originally the backyard of Via del Babuino's *palazzi*, this cobbled alley is home to art galleries and artisan workshops.

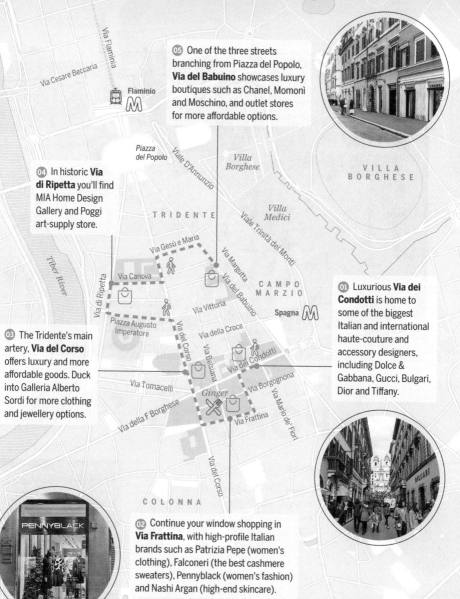

05 One of the three streets branching from Piazza del Popolo, **Via del Babuino** showcases luxury boutiques such as Chanel, Momonì and Moschino, and outlet stores for more affordable options.

04 In historic **Via di Ripetta** you'll find MIA Home Design Gallery and Poggi art-supply store.

01 Luxurious **Via dei Condotti** is home to some of the biggest Italian and international haute-couture and accessory designers, including Dolce & Gabbana, Gucci, Bulgari, Dior and Tiffany.

03 The Tridente's main artery, **Via del Corso** offers luxury and more affordable goods. Duck into Galleria Alberto Sordi for more clothing and jewellery options.

02 Continue your window shopping in **Via Frattina**, with high-profile Italian brands such as Patrizia Pepe (women's clothing), Falconeri (the best cashmere sweaters), Pennyblack (women's fashion) and Nashi Argan (high-end skincare).

Via Flaminia
Via Cesare Beccaria
Flaminio M
Piazza del Popolo
Viale D'Annunzio
Villa Borghese
VILLA BORGHESE
TRIDENTE
Villa Medici
Viale Trinità dei Monti
Tiber River
Via Gesù e Maria
Via Margutta
Via Canova
Via di Ripetta
Via del Babuino
CAMPO MARZIO
Via Vittoria
Spagna M
Piazza Augusto Imperatore
Via della Croce
Via del Corso
Via Belsiana
Via dei Condotti
Via Tomacelli
Via Borgognona
Ginger
Via Mario de' Fiori
Via della F Borghese
Via Frattina
Via del Corso
COLONNA
PENNYBLACK

N
0
0
400 m
0.2 miles

18

Explore Piazza del
POPOLO

ART | HISTORY | CHURCHES

▬▬▬ Crossing monumental Piazza del Popolo doesn't simply mean reaching the three main arterial roads of the city's Tridente neighbourhood. It's also the perfect occasion to dig deeper into Rome's ecclesiastic architecture and soak up its manifold artistic charms.

🗺 How to

Getting here and around Take the metro to Flaminio or Spagna, or a bus (61, 89). Walking is the best way to experience the square and the neighbourhood up to Piazza Venezia.

How much Church admission is free; it costs €2 to light up Caravaggio's painting.

Healthy meal Tucked away in Via Margutta, historic Il Margutta gourmet vegetarian restaurant offers a buffet-style lunch.

Imposing Gate

The perfect way to reach the piazza is to step over the threshold of the commanding Porta del Popolo gate, originally the ancient Porta Flaminia. From the always hectic traffic around Flaminio metro station, it feels liberating to enter a partially pedestrian area. The gate's exterior facade was completed by architect Giovanni Lippi, better known by the alias Nanni di Baccio Bigio, and the internal facade boasts work by Bernini and was embellished to celebrate the arrival in Rome of Christina of Sweden.

Marble Heart

Planning for this striking urban portal to Rome began in the 16th century with the positioning of what's known as the Flaminio Obelisk, the first obelisk to be brought to the

👓 Views From Above

The single best view over Piazza del Popolo can be enjoyed from Villa Borghese. Right behind the fountain of the Goddess Roma is the Pincio Terrace, which offers arguably the area's best urban walk. From here a fantastic 180-degree panorama over the square unfolds.

Left Chigi Chapel, Basilica di Santa Maria del Popolo (p92) **Above left** Piazza del Popolo **Above right** Fontana del Nettuno (p93)

city. Some 24m tall, it was moved here from the Circus Maximus by Pope Sixtus V in 1589. The modern-day elliptical square is the work of 19th-century architect Giuseppe Valadier, who also designed the large fountain, featuring marble basins and water-gushing lions.

Sacred Architecture

Before you venture into lively Via del Corso, artsy Via Ripetta and trendy Via del Babuino, make time for the gorgeous 15th-century Basilica di Santa Maria del Popolo, on your left as you pass through the gate. Step inside the church to see masterpieces such as the Chigi Chapel, designed by Raphael and completed by Bernini in the late 17th century, the Cerasi Chapel, enshrining Caravaggio's *Conversion on the Way to Damascus* and *The Crucifixion of St Peter*, and Pinturicchio's frescoes decorating the Della Rovere Chapel. Admirers of sacred art and architecture can also visit the twin churches of 17th-century Santa Maria in Montesanto and Santa Maria dei Miracoli.

🚸 Da Vinci Museum

After you visit the Basilica di Santa Maria del Popolo, you can duck into the Leonardo da Vinci Museum (museodavinci.it), located right beside the church.

Creator, engineer, architect, artist, scientist, anatomist – Leonardo may well be the greatest genius the world has ever seen. The museum offers interactive life-size machines, a reproduction of Leonardo's studies, his anatomical sketches such as the famous Vitruvian Man, and a multimedia animation of *The Last Supper*. Even though it might seem to be aimed at kids, adults will be equally entertained, making this a perfect family experience.

Left Museo Leonardo da Vinci **Below** Flaminio Obelisk

By means of an optical illusion, the churches look identical, but they actually have different domes and layout.

Mighty Fountains

Framed by lush gardens and marble sculptures, Piazza del Popolo is sublime proof that Rome has never lacked public fountains. Apart from the central fountain surrounding the obelisk, you can pose for fantastic shots in front of two side fountains designed by Valadier and built by Giovanni Ceccarini.

On the eastern side is the Fontana della Dea di Roma (Fountain of the Goddess Roma), a large sculptural complex of the armed goddess with the two Roman rivers, the Tiber and the Aniene, and the she-wolf feeding Romulus and Remus at her feet. On the other side of the piazza, right in front, is the Fontana del Nettuno (Fountain of Neptune), where the god of the sea dominates a large basin, holding a trident in his right hand and flanked by tritons with dolphins.

Listings

Palaces & Museums

Palazzo del Quirinale

Seat of the Italian president, this historic palace has been used as residence, public office and place of worship since ancient times. Built by architects Fontana, Maderno and Bernini, it houses a superlative art collection.

Scuderie del Quirinale

Also known as Scuderie Papali, these former stables of Palazzo del Quirinale were built between 1722 and 1732 and are now the stunning venue for art exhibitions.

Palazzetto Zuccari

Known as 'monsters' house' for the decorations on its facade, Palazzetto Zuccari hosts one of the world's largest libraries about Italian art.

Galleria d'Arte Moderna

Set in an ancient cloister of the Discalced Carmelites, the Modern Art Gallery houses a rich collection of paintings, sculpture, drawings and engravings by major Italian artists of the 19th and 20th centuries.

Ara Pacis Museum

A modern building close to the Augustus Mausoleum, Museo dell'Ara Pacis houses the Altar of Peace, built after the emperor's wars beyond the Alps and in Spain, and hosts temporary exhibitions.

Villa Medici

This magnificent Renaissance villa has belonged to the Medici family since 1576. You can visit its elegant gardens, some internal halls and lodges, and contemporary exhibitions.

Domus Romane of Palazzo Valentini

In the underground levels of this mansion you can visit the excavations of several Roman patrician *domus* and see decorations, rooms, a kitchen and thermal baths, accompanied by multimedia presentations.

Palazzo Colonna

The 14th-century Palazzo Colonna was built over five centuries, allowing space for different artistic and architectural styles. Visit the gardens, the Princess Isabelle Apartment and the mesmerising Galleria Colonna.

Palazzo Borghese

Belonging to the powerful Roman Borghese family, this elegant palace boasts beautiful gardens, frescoes and a rich art collection. Today it houses the Galleria del Cembalo, which hosts interesting temporary exhibitions.

Museo delle Cere

Set in Palazzo Colonna, Rome's wax museum was launched in 1958 and displays hundreds of figures of actors, singers, popes, scientists, musicians and more, from George Clooney to Albert Einstein.

GIVAGA/SHUTTERSTOCK ©

Palazzo del Quirinale

Spaghetti, Aperitivi & Wine

Il Piccolo Buco €€

Italian for 'little hole', Il Piccolo Buco serves traditional recipes with a personal twist. The long-risen pizza with high-quality toppings makes this place a favourite with locals.

Ginger €€

Cosy and laid-back Ginger in Via Borgognona serves healthy dishes such as vegan burgers, clam spaghetti and marinated tuna with rice.

Colline Emiliane €€

Tuck into the authentic recipes of the Emilia Romagna region in this cosy family restaurant – perfect if you're craving hearty meals of tortellini, lasagna and *tagliatelle*.

Harry's Bar €€€

Boasting a triumphant position near the Trevi Fountain, Harry's is a great place to round off a long but rewarding day. Try one of its famous cocktails as an *aperitivo* or tuck into some of its epicurean cuisine if you're hungry.

Fatamorgana €

The all-natural artisan gelato from Fatamorgana in Via Laurina is always worth a detour from Via del Corso. When in doubt, pick baklava, Bronte pistachio or ginger cream with lemon.

Enoteca Buccone €€

This historic wine cellar in Via Ripetta is known for its great selection of wine, spirits and beer. It also serves a light lunch and arranges tastings that include wine and finger food.

Arts & Faith

Basilica di Sant'Andrea delle Fratte

Fully renovated in the 17th century, the bell tower and dome of this ancient church are the work of architect genius Borromini, while the two angel sculptures were carved by Bernini.

Enoteca Buccone

Basilica di Sant'Andrea al Quirinale

A baroque gem designed by Gian Lorenzo Bernini, the stunning interior of this church is decorated with polychrome marble. The main chapel has a gilded-bronze altar adorned with lapis lazuli.

Chiesa di San Carlo alle Quattro Fontane

Devoted to Milan's Cardinal Borromeo, this church and its cloister were Borromini commissions. His typical style of moving lines and curves is visible on the small yet impressive facade.

Chiesa di Santa Maria della Vittoria

One of the greatest examples of Roman baroque, this church was designed by Carlo Maderno and beautifully decorated inside with masterpieces by leading artists such as Bernini and Guercino.

Unwind & Recharge

Hassler Hotel Spa

From sauna to massage, enjoy a luxury treatment at Hassler Hotel's Amorvero Spa to round off a long day of sightseeing. It's located on top of the Spanish Steps.

 Scan for more things to do in Tridente, Trevi & the Quirinale

VATICAN CITY, BORGO & PRATI

ART | ARCHITECTURE | HISTORY

Experience Vatican City, Borgo & Prati online

VATICAN CITY, BORGO & PRATI
Trip Builder

TAKE YOUR PICK OF MUST-SEES AND HIDDEN GEMS

Steeped in history and rich in art, this area boasts some of Rome's main highlights, including Michelangelo's stunning dome at St Peter's Basilica. Go beyond the tourist draws to discover the eateries of stylish Prati and wander the alleys of Borgo.

🔯 Neighbourhood Notes

Best for A combination of sacred and secular, modern architecture and great restaurants

Transport The closest metro stations are Cipro, Ottaviano and Lepanto.

Getting around Walking is the best way to enjoy the area's charms.

Tip Reach the highlights early in the morning to avoid long lines.

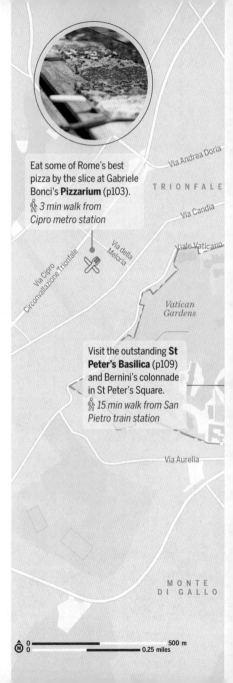

Eat some of Rome's best pizza by the slice at Gabriele Bonci's **Pizzarium** (p103).
🚶 *3 min walk from Cipro metro station*

Visit the outstanding **St Peter's Basilica** (p109) and Bernini's colonnade in St Peter's Square.
🚶 *15 min walk from San Pietro train station*

Via Andrea Doria

TRIONFALE

Via Candia

Viale Vaticano

Via della Meloria

Via Cipro

Circonvallazione Trionfale

Vatican Gardens

Via Aurelia

MONTE DI GALLO

0 — 500 m
0 — 0.25 miles

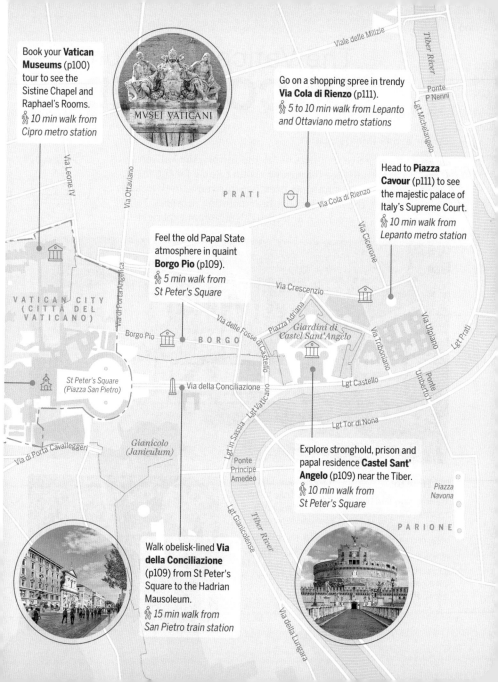

Book your **Vatican Museums** (p100) tour to see the Sistine Chapel and Raphael's Rooms.
🚶 *10 min walk from Cipro metro station*

MVSEI VATICANI

Go on a shopping spree in trendy **Via Cola di Rienzo** (p111).
🚶 *5 to 10 min walk from Lepanto and Ottaviano metro stations*

Head to **Piazza Cavour** (p111) to see the majestic palace of Italy's Supreme Court.
🚶 *10 min walk from Lepanto metro station*

Feel the old Papal State atmosphere in quaint **Borgo Pio** (p109).
🚶 *5 min walk from St Peter's Square*

Explore stronghold, prison and papal residence **Castel Sant' Angelo** (p109) near the Tiber.
🚶 *10 min walk from St Peter's Square*

Walk obelisk-lined **Via della Conciliazione** (p109) from St Peter's Square to the Hadrian Mausoleum.
🚶 *15 min walk from San Pietro train station*

Viale delle Milizie
Tiber River
Ponte P Nenni
Lgt Michelangelo

Via Leone IV
Via Ottaviano
PRATI
Via Cola di Rienzo
Via Cicerone
Via Ulpiano
Lgt Prati

VATICAN CITY
(CITTÀ DEL VATICANO)
Via di Porta Angelica
Via della Fossa di Castello
Via Crescenzio
Piazza Adriana
Giardini di Castel Sant'Angelo
Via Triboniano
Ponte Umberto I

Borgo Pio
BORGO
St Peter's Square (Piazza San Pietro)
Via della Conciliazione
Lgt Vaticano
Lgt Castello
Lgt Tor di Nona

Gianicolo (Janiculum)
Via di Porta Cavalleggeri
Lgt in Sassia
Lgt Sassia
Ponte Principe Amedeo
Piazza Navona
PARIONE

Via Gianicolense
Tiber River
Via della Lungara

19 The Vatican Museums UNCOVERED

ART | HISTORY | CHRISTIANITY

▰▰▰ Gathering five centuries of art and history, the Vatican Museums are a must-see for anyone visiting Rome for the first time (or the second). Sprawling over 7km and home to thousands of masterpieces, the museums can be a daunting prospect. Follow our suggestions to create an unforgettable museum experience.

Sala degli Animali

SILVERFOX999/SHUTTERSTOCK ©

🗺 How to

Getting here Take the metro to Ottaviano or Cipro, or a bus (23, 49, 492) or tram (19).

When to go Book a private tour before or after closing time for crowd-free visits.

Special tours Check the official website for special tours: tickets.musei vaticani.va/home.

Private tours Contact Take Walks (takewalks. com/rome-tours) or the Roman Guy (theroman guy.com).

OPACHEVSKY IRINA/SHUTTERSTOCK ©

Left Sistine Chapel **Far left top** Hall of the Animals **Far left bottom** Painted ceiling, Raphael Rooms

VATICAN CITY, BORGO & PRATI EXPERIENCES

Paintings Visitors rush to the Sistine Chapel, featuring artist genius Michelangelo's world-famous 16th-century frescoes commissioned by Pope Julius II. Take your time to admire *The Last Judgment*, decorating the wall behind the main altar, and the stunning ceiling portraying the stories of Genesis, the prophets and the sibyls. Near the Sistine Chapel, don't miss the mesmerising Gallery of Maps, home to 40 large-scale maps by cosmographer Ignazio Danti. The other big draw is Raphael's Rooms, featuring work by the renowned painter, commissioned by Julius II to decorate his apartment.

Sculpture After the entrance, in the Pio Clementino Museum's Octagonal Court, marvel at sculptural wonders *Laocoön* (c 40–30 BCE), the *Belvedere Apollo* (c 150 CE) and Antonio Canova's *Perseus Triumphant* (1800–01). Other sculptural highlights, also part of the Pio Clementino Museum, include the Gallery of the Candelabra, the Hall of the Muses and the Hall of Animals.

History History buffs can enjoy an overdose of relics, artefacts, monuments and archaeological finds in the Etruscan Museum and Egyptian Museum, both founded by Pope Gregory XVI in the 19th century. Also worth a visit is the fascinating Gregoriano Profano Museum, also founded by Gregory XVI. The collection explores ancient pagan times, with finds including bas-reliefs, mosaics and statues from Rome and surrounding cities such as Veio, Cerveteri and Ostia.

◇ Hidden Gems

Devote at least five hours to your visit to the Vatican Museums, and be sure to make time for these two hidden gems.

The little-visited 150m-long **Carriage Pavilion** (accessible with a regular ticket) retraces the history of papal mobility. See the opulent 19th-century grand gala carriage and the Nuova Campagnola Fiat where Pope John Paul II was shot in 1981. The **Armoury of Urban VIII**, in the Old Hall of the Swiss Guard, displays the beautiful set of Julius II's papal armour and the tournament armour of Constable Charles of Bourbon. Book through the official website.

Recommended by Sandro Barbagallo, *curator of the Vatican Museums' Department of Historical Collections*

20 Vatican City
VICTUALS

VATICAN CITY, BORGO & PRATI EXPERIENCES

TRADITION | PIZZA | GELATO

The restaurants around the Vatican can cater to the most demanding palates. From homely trattorias serving hearty classics rooted in *cucina povera* (peasant food) to pizzerias dishing up crisp slices heavy in seasonal toppings, you'll enjoy finding your neighbourhood favourites.

🍽 How to

Getting here Take the metro to Cipro, Ottaviano or Lepanto, or a bus (40, 64, 70, 81, 490).

Prices A restaurant meal costs €15 to €30 per person. A whole pizza costs from €8 and pizza by the slice from €3, depending on toppings and weight. Gelato starts at €3.

Food shopping Bring home some Roman tradition by stocking up at the Mercato Trionfale, open daily.

Tip Follow seasonality to find the best quality.

Far left top Alfresco dining, Borgo Pio
Far left bottom *Maccheroni alla gricia*

Choose Your Treat

Traditional Between Prati and Trionfale travellers can enjoy all the Roman classics, from *cacio e pepe* pasta to *coda alla vaccinara* (oxtail stew). Head to homely Trattoria del Gallo Brillo for unforgettable *rigatoni amatriciana* and tiramisu, Hostaria Dino e Tony for its *gricia* (*amatriciana* minus tomato) and Osteria dell'Angelo for a perfect carbonara. Those up for daring combinations will find a very personal take on tradition at L'Arcangelo near Piazza Cavour.

Pizza You won't have to go far for a great pizza. Under the mighty shade of the Vatican's walls, Gabriele Bonci's Pizzarium dishes out light, crunchy slices of goodness with an ever-changing selection of toppings. Not far away, La Pratolina and Pinsa 'mpò serve the oval-shaped Roman pizza (or better, *pinsa*) outdoors or take away. Osteria di Birra del Borgo's chef Luca Pezzetta is known for the quality of his dough, topped with carefully selected seasonal ingredients.

Gelato There's a reason Neve di Latte is one of Rome's best gelaterias: it uses biodynamic milk, organic eggs, seasonal fruit and high-quality hazelnuts, pistachios, almonds, peanuts and walnuts. The good news is that it's not alone: in the same neighbourhood you can sample the all-natural gelato of Gelateria dei Gracchi; Hedera, in Borgo Pio; and Al Settimo Gelo, near Piazza Mazzini.

🍸 Aperitivo in Prati

Whet your appetite in these venues around Prati with an early-evening *aperitivo* made up of fizzy cocktails, craft beer and gourmet delights.

Aqualunae This new bistrot offers an enticing pre-dinner *aperitivo* with cocktails and seven sophisticated finger-food tastings to be enjoyed indoors or alfresco.

Tomà Off busy Via Cola di Rienzo, this *osteria*-style restaurant serves hungry customers appetising nibbles in its intimate interior and pleasant outdoor area after 6pm.

Le Carré Français A slice of Paris in Rome: for aperitif, Le Carré Français showcases platters of cold cuts and cheese, *boulangerie* treats and French wines.

21

Delve Beneath
ST PETER'S

HISTORY | ARCHAEOLOGY | CHRISTIANITY

Everybody knows St Peter's Square and its basilica, but not as many are aware that a whole universe hides beneath. Built beside Caligula's Circus, today's Renaissance basilica is a modern place of worship atop a 4th-century Constantinian basilica. Journey to the underworld to unearth the secrets of an ancient Roman cemetery and the foundation of St Peter's.

🏛 How to

Getting here Take the train to Stazione San Pietro, the metro to Ottaviano or bus 64.

Cost A single ticket, including local guide, is €13.

Bookings Email scavi@fsp.va, or show up at nearby Ufficio Scavi, and give your details (name, group size, preferred language) and best contact method.

Come prepared The underground area is humid and has stairs.

Caligula's Circus The original Constantinian basilica was erected in the 4th century beside Caligula's Circus, built in 37 CE on the site of the Horti Agrippinae, the gardens and villa of his mother, Agrippina. Early Christians were executed at the circus, and it's said that

St Peter was among them. The circus was soon occupied by graves that couldn't be accommodated in the nearby necropolis.

Roman cemetery Roughly underneath the current basilica's main nave is a huge Roman graveyard, in use for more than 350 years from

Above Tomb of Pope Paul VI
Right top St Peter's Baldachin
Right bottom Tomb of Pope Pius XI

NOMADFRA/SHUTTERSTOCK ©

The Mystery of St Peter's Grave

In excavations between 1939 and 1950 St Peter's grave was found to be empty. Further excavations unearthed a small box containing bone fragments belonging to a 60- to 70-year-old man, but no foot bones. It's said that Peter was crucified upside down, which would separate the feet from the rest of the body.

Augustus to Constantine. As you walk along its alleys, you can see the transition from paganism to Christianity in the symbols and architecture of its mausoleums.

St Peter's tomb When Constantine built his basilica on top of the Roman necropolis, he took care by means of extensive terracing not to destroy the graves. On the eastern side, 7m below the altar of the Renaissance basilica, is a mosaic-floored area with a red wall and a niche known as the Gaius Trophy, erected to protect and mark what were believed to be St Peter's remains. This thus became a pilgrimage site even before the time of Constantine, the first Christian emperor.

ST PETER'S
Art & Architecture

01

02

03

04

05

06

01 Facade of St Peter's Basilica

Designed by Carlo Maderno, the 17th-century facade displays an upper section with 13 lined-up statues: Christ, John the Baptist and 11 apostles.

02 La Pietà

Created by Michelangelo when he was 25, *La Pietà* represents a young Mary holding her dead son.

03 Fountains of St Peter's Square

The twin fountains are the masterpieces of two major 17th-century artists: Carlo Maderno and Bernini.

04 St Peter's and St Paul's Statues

St Peter holds two keys in his right hand; St Paul holds a sword in his right hand, a book in his left.

05 St Peter's Square

A mesmerising colonnade frames the square, anchored by an Egyptian obelisk.

06 St Peter's Dome

Designed by Michelangelo and completed by Giacomo della Porta and Domenico Fontana.

07 St Peter's Baldachin

Bernini's majestic baroque bronze canopy stands atop the main altar and the alleged site of St Peter's tomb.

07

08

09

11

10

12

08 Chair of St Peter
Bernini's grand monument enshrines the wooden chair that tradition says belonged to St Peter, the first pope.

09 Monument to Alexander VII
Bernini's monumental marble sculpture shows

four female statues of the virtues and the praying pope on top.

10 Monument to Clement XIII
Canova's grand three-level masterpiece shows two lions, statues of Death and Religion, Clement XIII's

sarcophagus and the pope kneeling in prayer.

11 Transfiguration Mosaic
The mosaic is a famous reproduction of Raphael's painting *The Transfiguration,* kept in the Pinacoteca Vaticana.

12 Bronze Statue of St Peter
This tall statue shows St Peter giving a blessing with his right hand and holding the keys to Heaven on his left.

22

The Rome of the
POPES

WALKING TOUR | HISTORY | ART

▬▬▬ Follow in the footsteps of popes, cardinals and bishops when Rome was the heart of the Papal States. Get lost in the maze of narrow alleys and discover the original streets, palaces and prisons of the bygone Papal Kingdom.

LUCAMATO/SHUTTERSTOCK ©

🗺 Trip Notes

Getting here Take the metro to Ottaviano and Lepanto, or bus 40, 62 or 64.

How much To climb St Peter's dome costs €10; admission to the Hadrian Mausoleum is €15.

Gelato stop Enjoy an artisan gelato at Hedera in Borgo Pio.

Hidden gem Passetto di Borgo (pictured above), the secret passageway popes used to reach Castel Sant'Angelo when in danger in the Vatican, runs along Borgo Sant'Angelo.

🏛 Recalling the Spina di Borgo

Mussolini's project the Via della Conciliazione (built 1936–50) required the demolition of a thorn-shaped medieval quarter known as the Spina di Borgo. Many locals remember taking in a view of St Peter's Square after crossing the *spina's* charming cluster of narrow alleys past Renaissance buildings.

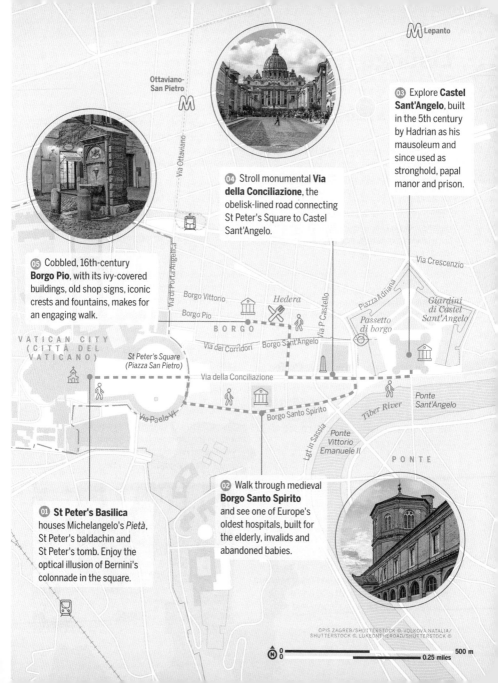

Ottaviano-
San Pietro
Ⓜ

Via Ottaviano

03 Explore **Castel Sant'Angelo**, built in the 5th century by Hadrian as his mausoleum and since used as stronghold, papal manor and prison.

04 Stroll monumental **Via della Conciliazione**, the obelisk-lined road connecting St Peter's Square to Castel Sant'Angelo.

05 Cobbled, 16th-century **Borgo Pio**, with its ivy-covered buildings, old shop signs, iconic crests and fountains, makes for an engaging walk.

Via di Porta Angelica

Borgo Vittorio

Borgo Pio

Hedera

Via P Castello

Via Crescenzio

Piazza Adriana

Giardini di Castel Sant'Angelo

Passetto di borgo

B O R G O

Via dei Corridori   Borgo Sant'Angelo

VATICAN CITY
(CITTÀ DEL
VATICANO)

St Peter's Square
(Piazza San Pietro)

Via della Conciliazione

Via Paolo VI

Borgo Santo Spirito

Tiber River

Ponte Sant'Angelo

01 St Peter's Basilica
houses Michelangelo's *Pietà*, St Peter's baldachin and St Peter's tomb. Enjoy the optical illusion of Bernini's colonnade in the square.

Lgt in Sassia

Ponte Vittorio Emanuele II

P O N T E

02 Walk through medieval **Borgo Santo Spirito** and see one of Europe's oldest hospitals, built for the elderly, invalids and abandoned babies.

Ⓝ 0
  0
500 m
0.25 miles

Listings

BEST OF THE REST

Churches & Museums

Chiesa Sacro Cuore del Suffragio

At this rare example of neo-Gothic ecclesiastic architecture in Rome, you can visit a museum devoted to holy souls stranded in purgatory.

Santa Maria in Traspontina Basilica

Often unnoticed due to its proximity to St Peter's, Santa Maria in Traspontina is a treasure trove of masterpieces by baroque artists including Carlo Fontana.

Leonardo da Vinci Experience

Go on a fascinating journey through the inventions of the Renaissance genius thanks to a multimedia exhibition showing his machines and paintings reproduced using the techniques and materials of Leonardo's time.

Amatriciana, Burgers & Coffee

Il Sorpasso   €€

Open all day from early morning, Il Sorpasso delivers an appealing *aperitivo* of finger foods and tastings paired with a good choice of cocktails and a rich wine list.

Gli Esploratori   €€

An innovative literary restaurant and wine bar, Gli Esploratori serves traditional Italian dishes with a twist. From carbonara with artichokes to bream linguine, the menu changes depending on what regions the kitchen is exploring.

Argot Prati   €€

With rustic-chic decor, this cocktail bar near Piazza Cola di Rienzo offer healthy bowls and gourmet burgers for lunch and fine dining in the evening, all ambitiously paired with signature cocktails.

L'Arcangelo   €€€

At his gourmet bistrot chef Arcangelo Dandini adds an appetising spin to regional recipes. Try tagliolini with butter, anchovies and spices, or roasted squid with cured meat and hazelnuts.

Camillo B   €€

Open every day from early morning, this large restaurant near Piazza Cavour serves sweet and savoury options for breakfast, a rich à la carte menu and an array of pizzas.

Sciascia Caffè 1919   €

In business for more than a century, Sciascia Caffè is a favourite breakfast stop. Try the luscious chocolate espresso, a slushy granita or an *aperitivo* of finger food and cocktails.

Freeda   €€

Bistrot and cocktail bar Freeda is a draw for *aperitivo* fans. An array of finger foods and platters of cured meats and cheeses are paired with artisan beer and good wines.

Lievito Pizzeria   €€

Using Stefano Callegari's time-honoured recipe for the dough and adding rich toppings in original combinations, Lievito is one of the most popular pizzerias in Prati.

ELENA POMINOVA/SHUTTERSTOCK ©

Mercato Trionfale

Carter Oblio €€€

Feel the *hygge* vibe of this modern restaurant, where Scandi style can be found as much in the decor as in the creative dishes. Try fried squid with borage or mirin-drizzled cod brûlée.

Flower Burger €

The colourful fare at Italy's first vegan fast-food burger joint (born in Milan) lures everyone in. Strictly all natural, it serves buns stuffed with plant-based patties, fresh and grilled vegetables, and tasty sauces.

Orto €

Located near Italy's Supreme Court, Orto is a must for foodies with a taste for variety. Its ever-changing lunch-buffet menu offers an array of veg delights from pasta to rich salads.

 Walks & Views

Ponte Sant'Angelo

Cobbled, statue-lined Ponte Sant'Angelo connects the Hadrian Mausoleum with the historic centre on the opposite bank of the Tiber. From either end, the views make a perfect postcard of Rome.

Vatican Gardens

A peaceful green oasis within the Vatican's walls, the gardens have been the papal place for rest and meditation since 1279. Book a tour to see the garden's fountains and rare plants.

Vicolo del Campanile

Off Via della Conciliazione, enter Vicolo del Campanile to see typical 15th-century architecture. The infamous dweller of civic 4 was Giovan Battista Bugatti, also known as Mastro Titta, longtime executioner for the Papal States.

Piazza Cavour

Surrounded by elegant buildings and great eateries, this large piazza offers a view of the Palace of Justice, the statue of Risorgimento leader Cavour and the Waldensian church.

Liberty Walk

Far from the busy main roads, a walk along Via Virginio Orsini, Via dei Gracchi and Via Alessandro Farnese will reveal Liberty-style houses decorated with frescoes and floral patterns.

 Markets & Fashion

Via Cola di Rienzo

On this upmarket shopping street, after you've checked out brands like Trussardi, Armani and Twinset, venture into alleys such as Via Germanico and Via Fabio Massimo for lovely shops and innovative eateries.

Via Ottaviano

Shop-lined Ottaviano, teeming with visitors on their way to St Peter's Square, connects Prati with the Vatican. Explore international flavours at Castroni deli and go window shopping for clothes and lingerie.

Mercato Trionfale

A favoured spot for local grocery shopping, this huge covered market has stalls overflowing with food-lovers on the lookout for cured meat, fresh pasta and street food.

Mercato dell'Unità

Built in 1928, Mercato dell'Unità's neoclassical facade and monumental gate make it an iconic stop. Though sometimes overpriced, it's famous for seasonal vegetables and locally sourced meat.

 Scan for more things to do in Vatican City, Borgo & Prati

MONTI, ESQUILINO & SAN LORENZO

ART | SHOPPING | MARKETS

Experience
Monti,
Esquilino &
San Lorenzo
online

MONTI, ESQUILINO & SAN LORENZO
Trip Builder

TAKE YOUR PICK OF MUST-SEES AND HIDDEN GEMS

▬▬ This triad of Roman neighbourhoods is one of the most vibrant parts of the city, rich in surprising sights, and with an attractive blend of cultures, history and traditions. The area is buzzing with life from early morning until late at night.

🗺 Neighbourhood Notes

Best for Stunning details mixing modern and traditional Roman features

Transport Take the metro to Cavour, or tram 5.

Getting around Walking and cycling are both great options.

Street art Enjoy the artworks' raw vibe set off against Rome's historical backdrop.

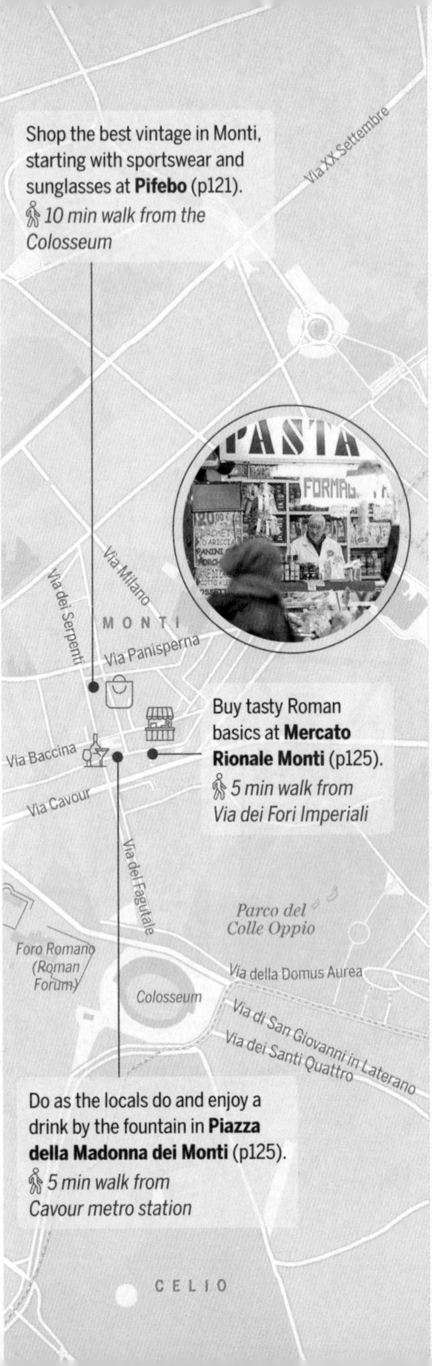

Shop the best vintage in Monti, starting with sportswear and sunglasses at **Pifebo** (p121).
🚶 10 min walk from the Colosseum

Buy tasty Roman basics at **Mercato Rionale Monti** (p125).
🚶 5 min walk from Via dei Fori Imperiali

Do as the locals do and enjoy a drink by the fountain in **Piazza della Madonna dei Monti** (p125).
🚶 5 min walk from Cavour metro station

Via XX Settembre
Via Milano
Via dei Serpenti
Via Panisperna
M O N T I
Via Baccina
Via Cavour
Via dei Fagutale
Foro Romano (Roman Forum)
Colosseum
Parco del Colle Oppio
Via della Domus Aurea
Via di San Giovanni in Laterano
Via dei Santi Quattro
C E L I O

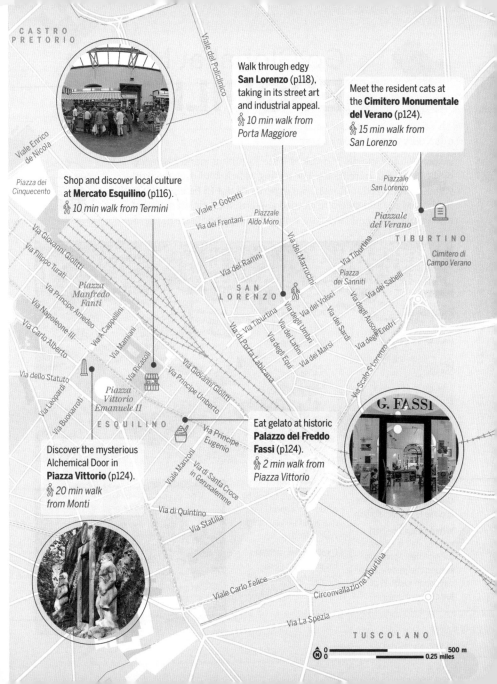

CASTRO PRETORIO

Walk through edgy **San Lorenzo** (p118), taking in its street art and industrial appeal.
🚶 *10 min walk from Porta Maggiore*

Meet the resident cats at the **Cimitero Monumentale del Verano** (p124).
🚶 *15 min walk from San Lorenzo*

Piazza dei Cinquecento

Shop and discover local culture at **Mercato Esquilino** (p116).
🚶 *10 min walk from Termini*

Viale Enrico de Nicola

Viale del Policlinico

Viale P Gobetti

Via dei Frentani

Piazzale Aldo Moro

Piazzale San Lorenzo

Piazzale del Verano

TIBURTINO

Cimitero di Campo Verano

Via Giovanni Giolitti

Via Filippo Turati

Via del Ramni

Via dei Marrucini

Via Tiburtina

Piazza dei Sanniti

Via Principe Amedeo

Piazza Manfredo Fanti

SAN LORENZO

Via degli Umbri

Via dei Volsci

Via dei Sardi

Via degli Ausoni

Via dei Sabelli

Via degli Enotri

Via Napoleone III

Via A. Cappellini

Via Mamiani

Via Tiburtina

Via dei Latini

Via degli Equi

Via dei Marsi

Via Carlo Alberto

Via di Porta Labicana

Via Scalo S. Lorenzo

Via dello Statuto

Via Ricasoli

Via Giovanni Giolitti

Via Principe Umberto

Piazza Vittorio Emanuele II

Via Leopardi

ESQUILINO

Via Buonarroti

Discover the mysterious Alchemical Door in **Piazza Vittorio** (p124).
🚶 *20 min walk from Monti*

Eat gelato at historic **Palazzo del Freddo Fassi** (p124).
🚶 *2 min walk from Piazza Vittorio*

G. FASSI

Via Principe Eugenio

Via Manzoni

Via di Santa Croce in Gerusalemme

Via di Quintino

Via Statilia

Viale Carlo Felice

Circonvallazione Tiburtina

Via La Spezia

TUSCOLANO

N
0   500 m
0   0.25 miles

23 Go Global at Mercato
ESQUILINO

CULTURES | FOOD | LOCAL LIFE

■■■■ Colours, smells and voices – the Esquilino market is made of these special ingredients. The feeling of being all over the world yet also immersed in Rome is an experience not to be missed. From fresh produce and spices to canned goods and fabric, this market has a wonderful ambience you won't find anywhere else in the city.

🗺️ How to

Getting here The market is close to Termini station.

When to go The best time to visit is either early in the morning or around the middle of the day, when lunch is in full swing.

Bring cash You won't always be able to pay by card – it's a good idea to ask before you make your selection.

Capture the moment Esquilino is a great subject for vibrant and varied photographs.

Navigating the market Being a delightful international hub of cultures and tastes, the Esquilino Market holds many wonderful surprises, but sometimes walking through it can be quite bewildering. Relax: getting distracted is key, and the real fun of this place.

Spices Stalls full of warm-coloured spices, beans and dried fruit welcome you as you make your way across from the main entrance door. Buy spices by the gram or dried fruit for a quick snack on the go.

Italian delicacies Although the international influence here is the main player, Italian staples such as olives, salami, *pizza bianca,* bread and delicious marinated vegetables can also be found. It's truly fascinating to try these foods in different combinations to see how they all blend with each other.

Fabric The market is divided into two buildings facing each other. While one is completely devoted to food, the other has a surprising side: fabric – of every kind, colour and structure. Glimpses of tailors at work surrounded by bright-coloured backdrops are a wonder to see.

Surprising produce Esquilino has the beauty and the luck to be a wonderful concoction of produce you won't find easily anywhere else in the city (apart from a few international shops in the suburbs, which mostly sell canned goods). It's a true paradise for food lovers.

Above left Globe artichokes **Far left top** Grains and pulses for sale **Far left bottom** Mercato Esquilino tailor

Then & Now

For more than 100 years this market was held in Piazza Vittorio and sold only Roman products, such as *pecorino* (sheep's milk cheese) and porchetta (roast pork). Many Romans still refer to it as 'the market of Piazza Vittorio' and not Esquilino.

Esquilino changed over the years, becoming a welcoming place for international cultures. It's the only market in Rome that caters to a range of customs and traditions.

Be sure to head outside, too: you'll find plenty more shops where you can purchase international goods.

24 The San Lorenzo SCENE

STREET ART | DRINKING | WALKS

■■■■ Welcome to San Lorenzo, where street art, nightlife, food, architecture and the authentic Roman lifestyle come together, day after day, to create an incomparable vibe. The raw allure and dazzling atmosphere of this neighbourhood give Rome a side that you might not have expected. From morning to evening, San Lorenzo never sleeps and it's always ready to amaze.

GIULIO NAPOLITANO/BLOOMBERG VIA GETTY IMAGES ©

🗺 How to

Getting here Take the metro to Policlinico or Termini, or tram 19.

When to go Watch local life bustle and hum around you in the morning, or enjoy an *aperitivo* in the evening.

Fuel up Head to Panificio Livio (Via Tiburtina 119) for a slice of *pizza rossa*, the classic mid-morning Roman snack.

Take a break Villa Mercede offers a small slice of nature amid the busy streets.

ELISA COLAROSSI/LONELY PLANET ©

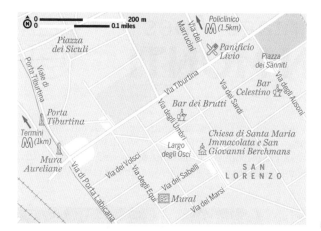

Far left top Streetside cafes and bars **Far left bottom** Chiesa di Santa Maria Immacolata e San Giovanni Berchmans

San Lorenzo is the perfect blend of the current and the historical. Its unpolished look and urban architecture mixed with ancient Roman facades are hallmarks of the area. The nearby university means the neighbourhood hosts hundreds of students from all over Italy, and they help shape the ambience of San Lorenzo: young, dynamic and full of life.

During the day Porta Tiburtina and the Aurelian Walls give San Lorenzo its archaeological cred, but in the core of the neighbourhood, street art, little boutiques and cafes are the stars. The industrial vibe mixed with the classic warmth of Roman colours is eye-catching – keep your eyes peeled for amazing murals and unexpected details. The market and the Chiesa di Santa Maria Immacolata e San Giovanni Berchmans are other local treasures to visit.

At night The real San Lorenzo comes out around sunset. The piazzas come alive and the vibrant scene that makes this neighbourhood one of a kind takes over. For a local-approved evening, *aperitivo* on a bench with a bottle of beer or a take-away drink, then sit at a bar and eat Roman dishes or a slice of *pizza al taglio* before moving on for a cocktail on Piazza dell'Immacolata, Largo degli Osci or Piazza dei Campani.

Bars & Street Art

Bar Celestino (Via degli Ausoni 62) and Bar dei Brutti (Via dei Volsci 71) are the main places to gather, from *aperitivo* hour to late at night, from beers to cocktails. Groovy and homestyle, and with very fair prices, they draw regulars from all over the city.

Street art in San Lorenzo is bright and colourful. Topics are disparate, but politics, history and society are mainstays. Murals on the highest buildings commemorate the bombing of the neighbourhood in 1943. Don't miss the mural at the corner in Via dei Sabelli 36.

25 Vintage Vibes
IN MONTI

SHOPPING | ART | DESIGN

If you're looking for art, fashion, design and unique pieces to purchase, Monti is one of the best parts of Rome to visit. The attractive alleys of the neighbourhood, in the immediate proximity of the Colosseum, and the hip atmosphere combine to create the best shops – from secondhand clothes to design of every kind.

FRANCESCA PAGLIAI/SHUTTERSTOCK ©

🗺 How to

Getting here Take the metro to Cavour, or walk five minutes from the Colosseum.

When to go Shops here are commonly open all day, but some do still close for lunch.

Gone to the beach During summer (especially August), shops might be closed for vacation.

Street tribute At Via del Pozzuolo 65 a mural celebrates famous Roman football player Totti.

HEMIS/ALAMY STOCK PHOTO ©

Spazio Artigiano

Via Nazionale

Via del Boschetto

Via Milano

Via Cesare Balbo

Via Urbana

Via Cavour

Boschettotre

Via del Serpenti

Via Panisperna

Humana Vintage

Via dei Quattro Cantoni

Via Urbana

Via Cavour

Pifebo

MONTI

Sottobosco

Flamingo

Via degli Zingari

Cavour Ⓜ

Via Baccina

Via Leonina

Via Giovanni Lanza

King Size

Mercato Monti Urban Market

Via Cavour

Ⓝ 0 _____ 200 m
0 _____ 0.1 miles

Vintage clothes Stylish locals mean great vintage shopping. Start with the boss of it all: Pifebo (Via dei Serpenti 135), whose two shops perfectly embody what vintage is in Rome – its sunglasses are the best in town, not to mention its sportswear. For more extravagant attire, King Size (Via Leonina 81) is the pick, with glam dresses, puffy jackets and one-of-a-kind accessories. Try Humana Vintage (Via Cavour 102), specialising in the fabulous trio of the '70s, '80s and '90s. For a taste of luxury with a sprinkling of glamour and elegance, head to Flamingo (Via del Boschetto 123).

Design and more Jewellery, trinkets, design pieces, decor – in Monti everything is at your fingertips. Sottobosco (Via Baccina 40) has the best jewellery and gift ideas from all over the world. Also worth a stop is Boschettotre boutique (Via del Boschetto 3), which is all about quirky design and singular items for the home. For genuine Italian crafts, from ceramics to timber to jewellery, drop by Spazio Artigiano (Vicolo dei Serpenti 13). If you're in Rome at the weekend, look out for the Mercato Monti Urban Market (Via Leonina 46), where artisans of every kind gather to show and sell their work.

Far left top Shoppers, Via Urbana
Far left bottom Design and furniture store, Monti

 Snack Stop

Take the perfect break at Zia Rosetta (Via Urbana 54), where you can choose between 25-odd gourmet *panini* and another dozen specials – all creatively stuffed with unexpected combinations.

Tempting pick-me-up alternatives include Antico Forno Serpenti (Via dei Serpenti 122) for pizzette, bread and other classic Italian bakers' treats (including to-die-for *cannoli*) or Ce Stamo a Pensà (Via Leonina 81) for beers and fried deliciousness.

26 Looking Through A LENS

PHOTOGRAPHY | WALKING | VIEWS

Wandering around and taking photographs of a newly discovered part of a city makes any trip twice as interesting, especially when the area is full of secluded points of view and stupefying sudden vistas. Murals, wonderful alleys, Roman landscapes and local details: be sure to stroll with camera in hand.

STEFANO RAVERA/ALAMY STOCK PHOTO ©

📷 Trip Notes

Getting here Take the metro to Cavour or Termini.

When to go Head out early in the morning or in the golden hour of early evening to take advantage of the beautiful Roman light.

Do yourself a favour Wear comfortable shoes!

Tram ride Jump on vintage (and amusingly noisy) tram 5 to travel around Esquilino and San Lorenzo.

ⓘ Navigating Courtyards

Some buildings and their courtyards are guarded by a door attendant. Always greet them, and be sure to ask permission before you take photos. Read any signs on the door before you enter a building: *Proprietà Privata* means that you won't be allowed to enter.

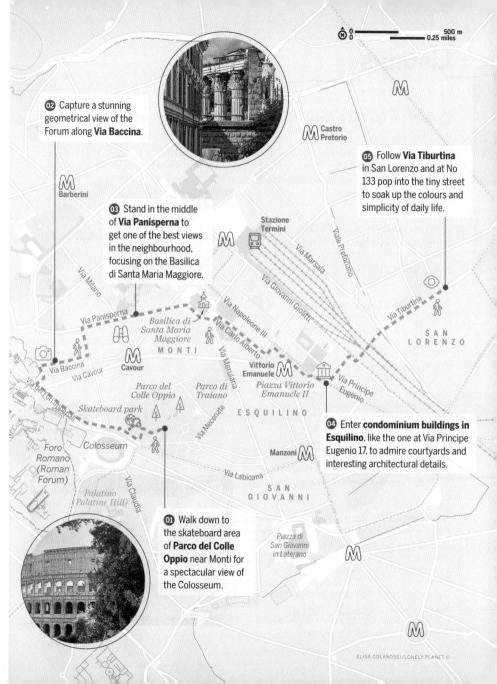

02 Capture a stunning geometrical view of the Forum along **Via Baccina**.

Castro Pretorio

05 Follow **Via Tiburtina** in San Lorenzo and at No 133 pop into the tiny street to soak up the colours and simplicity of daily life.

Barberini

03 Stand in the middle of **Via Panisperna** to get one of the best views in the neighbourhood, focusing on the Basilica di Santa Maria Maggiore.

Stazione Termini

Via Marsala

Via Giovanni Giolitti

Via Milano

Via Panisperna

Basilica di Santa Maria Maggiore

Via Napoleone III.

Via Carlo Alberto

Via Tiburtina

SAN LORENZO

Via Baccina

MONTI

Cavour

Via Cavour

Vittorio Emanuele

Via Merulana

Via Principe Eugenio

Piazza Vittorio Emanuele II

Parco del Colle Oppio

Parco di Traiano

ESQUILINO

04 Enter **condominium buildings in Esquilino**, like the one at Via Principe Eugenio 17, to admire courtyards and interesting architectural details.

Skateboard park

Via Mecenate

Manzoni

Foro Romano (Roman Forum)

Colosseum

Via Claudia

Via Labicana

SAN GIOVANNI

Palatino (Palatine Hill)

01 Walk down to the skateboard area of **Parco del Colle Oppio** near Monti for a spectacular view of the Colosseum.

Piazza di San Giovanni in Laterano

Listings

BEST OF THE REST

☕ Coffee at the Bar & Gelato

Bar Marani €

Drinking espresso while eating a *cornetto* (croissant) and reading the paper under the pergola in this San Lorenzo spot will become your favourite breakfast.

Bar dello Statuto €

Breakfast, *aperitivo* or a quick lunch with a *tramezzino*, this is the place to be: cool and fresh, while keeping alive the Roman vintage vibe in the heart of the neighbourhood.

Bar La Licata €

With one of the best views in Monti and a lively vibe, Bar La Licata makes a quick coffee or your drink of choice simply magnificent.

Antico Caffè del Brasile €

Stop for a quick break at this family-run historical location that will offer an authentic slice of bar life, plus homemade pastries and great coffee.

Fassi €

A keystone for locals, with some of the best gelato in town – try the *sampietrino* (cobble-stone; dedicated to the Roman road feature) in a cubic shape covered in chocolate.

Gelateria dell'Angeletto €

Two doors, a step, and an expo of ice-cream flavours will be the only thing you'll see. The place is tiny, but the taste is grand: fresh, genuine, creamy and truly homemade.

Fattori €

Gelato and more: this is the place for dessert lovers. The ice-cream flavours are sumptuous, and the small pastry bites deserve your attention too.

🚶 Surprising Walks

Cats in the Verano Cemetery

Walk quietly into the Cimitero Monumentale del Verano to find the cat sanctuary, whose many residents lead a peaceful life here. After years of the sanctuary's existence, the cats are the de facto guardians of the cemetery.

Alchemical Door in Piazza Vittorio

The newly renovated Piazza Vittorio is a wonderful place to visit. You can find a cat sanctuary, lots of green spaces and the mysterious Alchemical Door, a monument said to be a magical portal.

Porta Maggiore

The heart of Rome, traffic-wise: every Roman has passed through Porta Maggiore in their car at least once. The massive gate and the baker's tomb right in the middle make this a worthy destination.

Salita dei Borgia

This ravishing stairway is sometimes under-estimated by visitors to Monti. Make sure you at least glance at it.

Fassi

Parco del Colle Oppio

Magical at sunset and great for a little dose of nature between your walks in the city, the Parco del Colle Oppio is nonetheless at the centre of things. Look for the Colosseum peeking out at you.

🥂 Aperitivo in Monti

La Casetta a Monti   €€

If you walk by, you probably won't notice this little house fully covered with ivy. But its outdoor tables, ideal for an informal pre-dinner drink, come locally approved.

Rooftop Spritzeria Monti   €€

The stunning view here is accompanied by delicious tapas and even more delicious *spritz* – great for both stylish and more casual occasions.

La Bottega del Caffè   €

At this neighbourhood staple you can enjoy a sparkling *spritz* while watching local life go on in the main piazza.

Sit by a fountain

If you want to go authentic Roman, the best *aperitivo* can be had very simply: drink while sitting on the fountain's steps in Piazza della Madonna dei Monti.

🏛 Local Markets

Mercato di San Lorenzo

In the middle of the neighbourhood's main piazza, fruit and vegetable vendors can be found in a picturesque setting that's full of locals.

Mercato Rionale Monti

A true Roman market with all the basics, plus interesting regional and countrywide products to try on the spot or bring home.

Alchemical Door

🍴 Homestyle Roman Cuisine

Taverna dei Fori Imperiali   €€

The traditional dishes, the casual ambience and the homemade pasta are the three reasons this taverna is worth a visit, for lunch or dinner.

Vecchia Roma   €€

Tradition, taste and authenticity – this is the trattoria people dream of. *Cacio e pepe* (pasta with cheese and pepper) is made before your eyes in a huge wheel of *pecorino Romano* cheese.

Trattoria da Danilo   €€

A classic in the best possible sense: da Danilo's walls are covered with photos of celebrities and its style is rustic and unpretentious. The vibe is like the food: cosy and incomparable.

La Matriciana dal 1870   €€

Ever wondered what it was like to eat out in Rome in the past? La Matriciana, with its wonderful 1930s-style interiors and traditional Roman cuisine, gives you a glimpse.

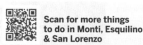

Scan for more things to do in Monti, Esquilino & San Lorenzo

MONTI, ESQUILINO & SAN LORENZO REVIEWS

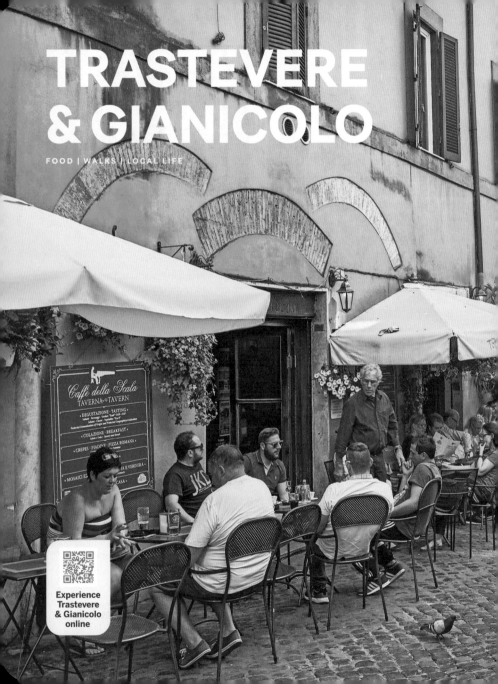

TRASTEVERE & GIANICOLO

FOOD | WALKS | LOCAL LIFE

Experience
Trastevere
& Gianicolo
online

TRASTEVERE & GIANICOLO
Trip Builder

TAKE YOUR PICK OF MUST-SEES AND HIDDEN GEMS

Trastevere and its surroundings offer splendid colours, rustic alleys and an authentic Roman vibe. The area's combination of tradition, beauty and modern life gives it a pure, wholehearted and surprising feel – you never know what you'll discover as you wander its lively streets.

🗺 Neighbourhood Notes

Best for An authentic and rustic essence, marvellous alleys, great food and local life

Transport Take tram 3 from Piazza Venezia.

Getting around The neighbourhood is great for walking and cycling.

Nightlife With lively streets full of locals, Trastevere is one of Rome's best neighbourhoods for a night out.

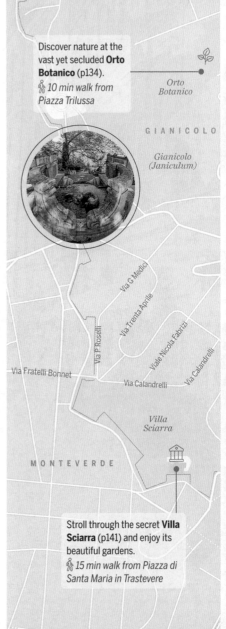

Discover nature at the vast yet secluded **Orto Botanico** (p134).
🚶 *10 min walk from Piazza Trilussa*

Orto Botanico

GIANICOLO

Gianicolo
(Janiculum)

Via G Medici

Via Trenta Aprile

Via P Roselli

Viale Nicola Fabrizi

Via Calandrelli

Via Fratelli Bonnet

Via Calandrelli

Villa Sciarra

MONTEVERDE

Stroll through the secret **Villa Sciarra** (p141) and enjoy its beautiful gardens.
🚶 *15 min walk from Piazza di Santa Maria in Trastevere*

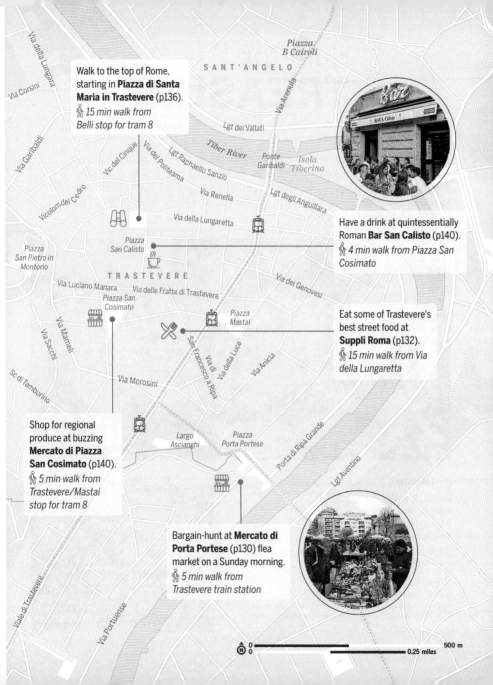

Walk to the top of Rome, starting in **Piazza di Santa Maria in Trastevere** (p136).

🚶 15 min walk from Belli stop for tram 8

Have a drink at quintessentially Roman **Bar San Calisto** (p140).

🚶 4 min walk from Piazza San Cosimato

Eat some of Trastevere's best street food at **Suppli Roma** (p132).

🚶 15 min walk from Via della Lungaretta

Shop for regional produce at buzzing **Mercato di Piazza San Cosimato** (p140).

🚶 5 min walk from Trastevere/Mastai stop for tram 8

Bargain-hunt at **Mercato di Porta Portese** (p130) flea market on a Sunday morning.

🚶 5 min walk from Trastevere train station

Hunt for
TREASURE

MARKET | VINTAGE | LOCAL CULTURE

Sunday morning in Rome means one thing: Porta Portese. The city's oldest flea market opens its doors from early in the morning to unveil its treasures – there's everything from expensive antiques to cheap trinkets. Hunting amid the clamour of local life for the best piece you can bring home will be a highlight of your trip.

PINO PACIFICO/REDA&CO/UNIVERSAL IMAGES GROUP VIA GETTY IMAGES ©

🗺 How to

Getting here Take the metro to Marconi, or bus 170 from Termini. Viale di Trastevere and Via Portuense are the market's main access points.

When to go The market is open Sunday from 6am to 2pm, but it is best to go early, when the best bargains are available.

Bring cash It's not possible to pay by card.

Consider your purchases Make sure that anything you buy is in good condition, and take your time – don't allow yourself to be pressured.

PINO PACIFICO/REDA&CO/UNIVERSAL IMAGES GROUP VIA GETTY IMAGES ©

Left Glassware stall **Far left top** Browsing for trinkets **Far left bottom** Comics for sale

An institution since 1945, Porta Portese takes its name from the nearby gate and spreads out over 2km. Romans and visitors gather here every Sunday morning to look for treasure, making this one of the most famous markets in Italy.

Bargain like a local Negotiating and talking are the two musts when you make a purchase. Don't be afraid to ask for a lower price or to joke around – it's all part of the experience. The vast array of people and things, the buzz of chatter and the flow of life around you are the perfect setting for a good bargaining session. Plunge in – and have fun!

What to buy There are more than 500 stalls selling just about everything: secondhand clothes, antiques, paintings, books, albums, cameras and more. Romans joke that you might even find an aeroplane! Buying well here is all about luck and having a good eye; the best stalls to approach have a chaotic blend of objects that you literally need to dig through.

Bring your camera Porta Portese is never the same from one week to the next. Every Sunday it accommodates new people, stalls and pieces, but somehow it always maintains its allure. It's a perfect place to photograph local life at its best and to really savour it.

 Local Tips

Cool stalls Look for the black-and-white cinema and TV stall selling posters, postcards and prints of Italian and international movies, TV shows and superstars. The owner is a fun, quirky guy who loves to chat. Also check out the very end of the market, where you'll find only locals. Stalls here sell old magazines, Rome-themed items (from Roma football team memorabilia to gadgets and books), decor, cameras, toys and things you didn't know you needed!

Authentic snack There's a food truck making tasty and filling porchetta sandwiches right in the heart of the market.

28 Street Food to **SAVOUR**

FOOD | TRADITION | CULTURE

▬▬▬ During a walk, after a night out, for a quick bite or just out of curiosity – it's always a good time to try Roman street food. It's the perfect way to dive into the local cuisine. Traditional dishes keep their essential flavours but are reinvented so they can be eaten fast.

🗺 How to

Getting here Jump on tram 3.

When to go Lunch, dinner, for a quick snack or for a different take on *aperitivo*.

Break up your walk Trastevere can easily be reached on foot if you're south of the centre.

Bakeries If you see the word *forno* be sure to go in and try something local and delicious.

Suppli Fast and delicious, Rome's most traditional street snack is *suppli*: fried risotto balls with tomato-sauce *ragù* and a heart of mozzarella. Eat yours at Suppli Roma (Via di San Francesco a Ripa 137) or Alari (Via Portuense 106d), the neighbourhood's two best *suppli* places.

Pizza Go for a mouth-watering slice of *pizza rossa* or *al taglio* (by the cut) at Casamanco (Via di San Cosimato 4) or for a rustic vibe at Pizzeria La Boccaccia (Via di Santa Dorotea 2).

Tramezzino This soft-bread sandwich with ham or tuna is commonly sold in bars

Right top *Maritozzi* **Right bottom** *Pizza al taglio*

🍨 **Sweet Street Treats**

Otaleg (Via di San Cosimato 14) – gelato spelt backwards – has traditional, innovative and even salty options (such as *cacio e pepe*); **Fior di Luna** (Via della Lungaretta 96) changes its flavours often, so it always has something new to try; and **Fatamorgana** (Via Roma Libera 11) is a Roman gelato institution.

throughout Italy, but in Trastevere you can find an extra-tasty Roman version at Trapizzino (Piazza Trilussa 46): *pizza bianca* dough in the shape of a triangle, filled with Rome's classic recipes.

Maritozzi Rome is famous for its *maritozzi* (sweet yeasty buns filled with freshly whipped cream). You can find them in any bar or pastry shop, but the best are at historic Il Maritozzaro (Via Ettore Rolli 50), in business since 1960 and open till late. Street-food devotees will be delighted to know that there's a savoury *maritozzo* too: try it at Il Maritozzo Rosso (Vicolo del Cedro 26).

TRASTEVERE & GIANICOLO EXPERIENCES

29 Botanical
BOUNTY

NATURE | GARDEN | WALKS

 Hidden in the heart of Trastevere, the 12-hectare Orto Botanico (Botanical Garden) is a literal discovery: even as you approach it you still can't quite see it. Spend some time here to get to know the nature-loving side of Rome and explore one of its vast green spaces.

🗺 **How to**

Getting here Take tram number 3.

When to go Visit in spring when the garden is in bloom.

Finding the garden Look for the big green gate at Largo Cristina di Svezia 23.

Wandering The garden's map has an itinerary, but you can always just explore as you like.

VALERIOMEI/SHUTTERSTOCK ©

The Roman botanical garden is a history- and nature-lover's paradise. Located at Villa Corsini, residence of Queen Cristina of Sweden in the second half of the 1600s, it's now run by the department of environmental biology at the Sapienza University of Rome.

Nature The generous grounds provide space for diverse plant and tree species. There are more than 40 kinds of palm tree, sections dedicated to ferns, roses and bamboo, and several varieties of grape, celebrating Italian regional wines. The breathtaking rock garden offers a

Above Japanese Garden **Right top** Scalinata Delle Undici Fontane **Right bottom** View of the Fontana dell'Acqua Paola

🚶 Tips for Visiting

Entering the Orto Botanico almost feels like walking in the countryside. It has pretty steep, winding paths, so wear comfortable shoes. You'll be able to drink from numerous tiny fountains for quick refreshment. Art installations can sometimes be found scattered through the grounds.

stunning view of the Fontana dell'Acqua Paola, just south of the Orto Botanico, and there's a calming Japanese garden and an interesting collection of medicinal plants. Greenhouses are home to tropical and aquatic species – the oldest greenhouse (Serra Corsini) hosts more than 200 species of cactus. A small Mediterranean forest has more than 300 kinds of century-old trees.

Fountains The Fontana dei Tritoni (1742), the first fountain you'll see upon entering the garden, is made of Carrara marble. Le Quattro Fontane (Four Fountains) are distributed throughout the garden, and the astonishing Scalinata Delle Undici Fontane (1742) has 11 spouts, the biggest shaped like the mouth of a dolphin.

30 Walk to the Top
OF ROME

VIEWS | WALKS | SIGHTS

The wonders of Rome will delight you all over again when you see them from different vantage points. On this walk you can discover the city from a whole new angle as you slowly reach its rooftops, taking in some stunning views along the way.

MAYDAYS/GETTY IMAGES ©

🗺 Trip Notes

Getting here Take tram 3.

Starting point Begin in Piazza di Santa Maria in Trastevere at what is believed to be the oldest fountain in Rome (pictured above), restored by Bernini in 1659 and Carlo Fontana in 1692.

When to go Avoid doing this walk between noon and 4pm in summer – it will be too hot.

Pretty alleys Vicolo del Cedro and Vicolo del Leopardo are two of the most beautiful alleys in Trastevere.

ⓘ Nasoni

Fill your water bottle at every *nasone* you encounter, as the further up the hill you go, the fewer fountains you'll find. This is especially recommended on a hot day. To drink like a Roman, put your finger on the faucet and drink from the little hole right on top.

05 The midday cannon salute in **Piazza Giuseppe Garibaldi** is a centuries-old tradition beloved by locals.

03 Have a sip of water at the Fontana di Via di Porta San Pancrazio before winding up the steps to **San Pietro in Montorio**, where you can see the Tempietto del Bramante.

GIANICOLO

Orto Botanico

Gianicolo (Janiculum)

Passeggiata del Gianicolo

02 Soak up Trastevere's stunning architecture in alleys such as **Vicolo del Cedro**.

Via Garibaldi

Vic del Leopardo

Via della Pelliccia

Piazza Sant'Egidio

Vicolo del Cedro

Via della Paglia

Largo Fumasoni Biondi

Via di Porta San Pancrazio

04 The spectacular **Fontana dell'Acqua Paola** is known locally as 'Fontanone' (Big Fountain). Peek at the view across the street from here.

Via G. Medici

Via Garibaldi

Piazza San Pietro in Montorio

TRASTEVERE

Via di San Cosimato

Via Luciano Manara

01 Start your walk in charming **Piazza di Santa Maria in Trastevere** home to one of the city's oldest basilicas.

Villa Sciarra

N 0 — 200 m
0 — 0.1 miles

Tiber River

DON'T LEAVE
Rome Without...

01

02

04

03

05

01 A Marble Name Tag from Il Marmoraro

Bring home a unique carved-marble name tag, handcrafted in one of the oldest shops in Via Margutta.

02 Roman Books from Libreria Cicerone

Buy unique and stunning books about Rome, new and second-hand, at this basement bookshop in front of Palazzo Chigi.

03 Jam and Chocolate at Castroni

Castroni has the best Italian candies, jams and chocolates in town, in three handy locations.

04 Linen from Gioren Biancheria

Aprons, tablecloths, bed linen and more: stock up on high-quality items for your kitchen or bedroom.

05 Cookies from Biscottificio Innocenti

The homemade *crostatine* and *tozzetti* here make a great gift.

06 Ceramics from De Sanctis dal 1890

This old shop in Rome has an impressive selection of lovely Italian ceramics.

07 Tote Bags and Socks from Elvis Lives

Every Roman has at least one item from this lively

shop, which sells items printed with Roman-dialect expressions.

08 Vintage Prints from Antiquario Piazza Borghese

These kiosks are full of interesting pieces, from books to vintage prints.

09 Wine from Les Vignerons

Specialises in locally sourced wines, often from small producers.

10 Cheese from Antica Caciara

For more than 100 years, this deli has offered the best regional produce and superb *pecorino Romano* cheese.

11 A Pen from Stilo Fetti

This paradise for pen aficionados has been in business since 1893. It also offers the option to have leather writing accessories personalised on the spot.

12 Coffee from Sant'Eustachio

One of the best coffees in Rome can be enjoyed at home, thanks to Sant' Eustachio's selection of beans and capsules.

Listings

BEST OF THE REST

 Coffee, Iced Tea or a Spritz

Bar San Calisto €

The style, the atmosphere, the people – this bar exudes Rome from every pore. Order a *spritz*, a homemade iced tea or a €1 ice cream on a scorching afternoon.

Caffè Settimiano €

In one of the best corners of Rome, framed by the Porta Settimiana, breakfasts and *aperitivi* look as though they've come out of a fairy tale.

Caffè Trastevere €

This historical bar with great coffee is located on a main road with plenty of shops. It's an ideal pit stop as you discover the two parts of the neighbourhood.

San Cosimato Caffè €

With a lively view of its piazza, this bar has great people-watching thanks to the market that takes place every morning from dawn.

✗ Trattorie & Osterie

Da Enzo al 29 €

One of the best trattorias in Trastevere, with a traditional setting, wonderful atmosphere and classic dishes served family style.

La Gattabuia €€

Romantically set, easy-going La Gattabuia has one of the city's best carbonaras.

Trattoria dal Cordaro €€

Authentic dal Cordaro has been serving the best Roman-style dishes since 1922. Enjoy the backyard and settle in like a local.

Trattoria da Augusto €

Feel as though you're dining at a friend's home as you enjoy the local cuisine at this proudly Roman trattoria.

L'Osteria della Trippa €€

Tradition with a sprinkle of creativity: Trippa takes its name from a classic Roman dish.

Otello €

Rustic-chic while keeping the much-loved trattoria atmosphere, Otello offers plenty of delicious local dishes, including the chocolate salami dessert.

Local Walks

Hidden Cloister

The stunning Chiesa di San Cosimato hides a real treasure: its marvellous cloister, which connects to a nearby hospital. It's a real must-see.

Mercato di Piazza San Cosimato

Shop, eat and watch how a Roman market works in one of the city's busiest piazzas. There's fish, fruit and regional delicacies to enjoy right on the spot.

Mercato di Piazza San Cosimato

Villa Sciarra

Camouflaged by buildings and large roads, this park is a jewel. Statues, fountains and the typical beauty of a Roman garden are there to be savoured.

Lungotevere

The longest bike path in Rome transforms into the famous annual Estate Romana on summer evenings, hosting a huge variety of stalls with street food, clothing and more.

Grattachecca

Villa Sciarra

Alla Fonte d'Oro   €

Since 1913 this kiosk has delivered the city's best *grattachecca* (shaved ice with syrup). Crowds of locals can be seen here late into the night on the hottest Roman evenings.

Sora Mirella   €

The second-oldest *grattachecca* kiosk in Rome has a cool location overlooking the Tiber. Try the delicious Lemon Cocco, with fresh coconut slices on top.

Beer, Pizza & Cocktails

Ivo a Trastevere   €

Real, thin Roman-style pizza in a very informal setting. Sit down and enjoy the family flavour and fun atmosphere.

Pizzeria Ai Marmi   €

Thin Roman pizza on thick marble tables – what's not to love? This rustic place has been in business since 1931.

Dar Poeta   €

This lively, well-known spot serves up traditional pizza and bruschetta. Eating here is a chance to take in an authentic Roman restaurant experience.

Freni e Frizioni   €

Once a car-repair shop, this cool spot for a pre- or post-prandial drink has become a landmark for locals. Sit outside for the true Roman vibe.

Santo Trastevere   €

Locals love this place for its excellent cocktails, served against a stylish but casual backdrop. There are good food options, too, from vegetarian to fish-based.

Ma Che Siete Venuti a Fà   €

The best beer in town can be had at this tiny but extremely cool spot. It can get crowded, and inside seats are limited – do as locals do and drink right outside.

Scan for more things to do in Trastevere & Gianicolo

SAN GIOVANNI & TESTACCIO

FOOD | HISTORY | CHURCHES

Experience
San Giovanni
& Testaccio
online

SAN GIOVANNI & TESTACCIO
Trip Builder

TAKE YOUR PICK OF MUST-SEES AND HIDDEN GEMS

███████ This pretty and authentically Roman area is loved by locals for its striking yet down-to-earth character. Stunning churches and architecture accompany traditional Roman food choices and a wealth of historical elements. The classic feel of Rome is definitely here, but in a new and inspiring setting.

🗺 Neighbourhood Notes

Best for Its unique and intriguing mix of ancient and very recently built surroundings

Transport Take the metro to Colosseo, San Giovanni or Piramide.

Getting around Walk, cycle or take the metro.

Nature break Stroll through the recently reopened Giardini di Via Sannio.

Discover romantic Aventino with its fragrant **Roseto Comunale** (p151).
🚶 15 min walk from Circo Massimo metro station

Eat your way around Testaccio, starting with pizza at **Panificio Passi** (p155).
🚶 10 min walk from Marmorata/Vanvitelli stop for tram 3

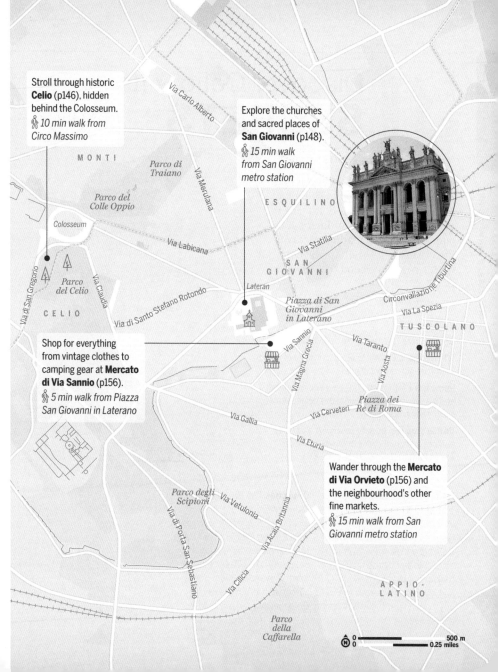

Stroll through historic **Celio** (p146), hidden behind the Colosseum.
🚶 *10 min walk from Circo Massimo*

Explore the churches and sacred places of **San Giovanni** (p148).
🚶 *15 min walk from San Giovanni metro station*

MONTI

Via Carlo Alberto

Parco di Traiano

Via Merulana

ESQUILINO

Parco del Colle Oppio

Colosseum

Via Labicana

Via Statilia

SAN GIOVANNI

Via di San Gregorio

Parco del Celio

Via Claudia

CELIO

Via di Santo Stefano Rotondo

Lateran

Piazza di San Giovanni in Laterano

Circonvallazione Tiburtina

Via La Spezia

TUSCOLANO

Shop for everything from vintage clothes to camping gear at **Mercato di Via Sannio** (p156).
🚶 *5 min walk from Piazza San Giovanni in Laterano*

Via Sannio

Via Magna Grecia

Via Taranto

Via Aosta

Via Gallia

Via Cerveteri

Piazza dei Re di Roma

Via Eturia

Wander through the **Mercato di Via Orvieto** (p156) and the neighbourhood's other fine markets.
🚶 *15 min walk from San Giovanni metro station*

Parco degli Scipioni

Via Vetulonia

Via di Porta San Sebastiano

Via Acaia Britannia

Via Cilicia

APPIO-LATINO

Parco della Caffarella

Ⓝ 0 —— 500 m
0 —— 0.25 miles

31 Discover Celio & Its **SECRETS**

WALKS | HISTORY | SIGHTSEEING

━━━━ Celio is one of the seven hills of Rome, with a secluded position and breathtaking surprises that make it something out of the ordinary. Ruins, churches and fascinating traces of history mean it's well worth venturing to this neighbourhood that seems lost in time.

🗺️ How to

Getting here Take the metro to Colosseo, or tram 3.

When to go Visit early to avoid crowds or at sunset for the magical atmosphere.

Rome base With interesting bars and restaurants and plentiful accommodation, this neighbourhood is a perfect place to stay.

Coffee stop Fuel up with delicious homemade pastries and great coffee at family-run Caffè Antica Roma.

Surrounded by an evocative complex of historical ruins and churches, Celio embodies what you'd expect from a walk around Rome. However, as it's hidden by the hulking majesty of the Colosseum, sometimes this part of the city doesn't get the attention it deserves.

Churches The Basilica di San Clemente is one of the finest examples of what's known as 'The Roman Lasagna' (a site that exposes different layers of history). The Basilica dei Santi Giovanni e Paolo offers a peek at the Temple of Claudius, hidden beneath its bell tower. And the Basilica

Right top Annunciation fresco, Basilica dei Santi Quattro Coronati **Right bottom** Porta San Sebastiano

🌿 Take a Nature Break

Celio's parks have plenty of history too. **Parco degli Scipioni** holds the remains of the mausoleum of the Scipiones, an influential aristocratic family of ancient Rome.

Occupied by vineyards during the Middle Ages, the superlative **Villa Celimontana** has wondrous gardens filled with traces of the past. You can see an Egyptian obelisk, the remains of the Basilica Hilariana sanctuary, three lovely fountains and several statues. It's a delightful place to visit at any time of year.

dei Santi Quattro Coronati houses ancient frescoes.

Ruins and gates Marvellous historical fragments can be seen here, from the Arco di Dolabella e Silano (an ancient gate recycled into an aqueduct) to the best-preserved part of the Aurelian Walls, including Porta San Sebastiano (the gate through which the Via Appia, the world's oldest highway, left the city) and Porta Latina. One of the most exciting locations is the Clivo di Scauro, an ancient street covered by the supporting arches of the 4th-century Basilica dei Santi Giovanni e Paolo. Beneath the basilica, at the Case Romane del Celio, you can see rooms that were used as houses and shops.

32 Admire Churches in
SAN GIOVANNI

WALKS | RELIGION | CULTURE

████ San Giovanni is one of the oldest neighbourhoods in Rome, with a unique mix of ancient ruins and modern architecture. Explore its churches and striking details to get to know the backbone of this multilayered city's fascinating culture and aesthetic.

SIRIO CARNEVALINO/SHUTTERSTOCK ©

🗺 How to

Getting here Take the metro to San Giovanni, or tram 3.

When to go Visit during the day for the local lifestyle.

Getting around San Giovanni is easily explored on foot.

History unearthed If you come by metro, look for the display of ancient artefacts at the new San Giovanni station, which were discovered during its construction.

KRAFTIA/SHUTTERSTOCK ©

Far left top Basilica di San Giovanni in Laterano **Far left bottom** Bronze statue of St Francis of Assisi

ⓘ Rome's Cathedral

The awe-inspiring Basilica di San Giovanni in Laterano is Rome's official cathedral and the pope's seat as the Bishop of Rome. It was originally commissioned by the Emperor Constantine and consecrated by Pope Sylvester I in 324 CE. From then until 1309, when the papacy moved to Avignon, it was the principal pontifical church, and the adjacent Palazzo Laterano was the pope's official residence. Both buildings fell into disrepair during the pope's French interlude and when Pope Gregory XI returned to Rome in 1377 he chose to move to the fortified Vatican.

Remember, if you're visiting the basilica, or any of Rome's churches and sacred places, be sure to cover your knees and shoulders before you enter. Always bring a scarf or a light jacket with you, even if it's summer.

The gentle giant Incredible inside and out, the Basilica di San Giovanni in Laterano (one of the four Papal Basilicas of Rome) overlooks the neighbourhood like a gentle giant. It's the oldest basilica in the world and truly majestic. Not far from it stand the Scala Sancta, 28 white-marble steps where it's said Jesus walked before he was interrogated by Pontius Pilate. St Helena brought the steps to Rome from Jerusalem.

The piazza The Aurelian Walls and the Porta San Giovanni are the perfect frame for the piazza. On 1 May a huge concert is held in the square to celebrate the Festa dei Lavoratori, which honours workers. The statue facing the basilica from the other side of the street is of St Francis of Assisi, patron saint of animals.

A church of Rome Just a few steps away, the Basilica di Santa Croce in Gerusalemme is one of the seven churches of Rome, the pilgrimage itinerary made famous by San Filippo Neri. Right next to the basilica, you can admire one of the city's most extraordinary gates, enriched by colourful glass stones. The gate gives access to the exclusive Orto Monastico, a private garden that you can only peep into from outside.

33 Romantic AVENTINO

WALKS | GARDENS | SIGHTSEEING

A peaceful slice of Rome, green and somehow fresher than the rest of the city (especially in summer), Aventino embraces you with its history, secluded nooks and delightful architecture. Locals have created a romantic feel to the neighbourhood that makes it a perfect setting for leisurely exploration.

BORIS-B/SHUTTERSTOCK ©

📷 How to

Getting here Take the metro to Circo Massimo, then walk for 10 minutes.

When to go In April you can enjoy the delicious scent of orange blossom.

Famous neighbour The area is within walking distance of the Colosseum.

The 'Great Beauty'

To fully comprehend the poetry of Aventino, watch Paolo Sorrentino's film *La grande bellezza*. The stunning opening scenes convey the neighbourhood's essence.

STRIPPEDPIXEL.COM/SHUTTERSTOCK ©

Far left top Roseto Comunale Far left bottom Fontana del Mascherone

A global rose garden The Roseto Comunale (open April to June only) has more than a thousand varieties of rose from all over the world. It's an essential visit if you're in town at the right time.

The Orange Garden Reached by walking up Via di Santa Marina Sabina from the Circo Massimo, the Parco Savello, more commonly known as the Giardino degli Aranci (Orange Garden), offers an unforgettable view. Locals and couples come here at sunset to make the most of the romantic atmosphere. Be sure to follow the cupola of St Peter's with your eye: the closer you come, the smaller it will appear. Don't miss the Fontana del Mascherone (1936), created from a 16th-century mask and an ancient bathtub taken from the city's archives.

Less visited treasures The fame of the neighbouring Orange Garden means the Giardino di Sant'Alessio is often overlooked, but it has an equally ravishing view (and is much quieter).

Students of history will appreciate the Basilica di Santa Sabina (built between 422 and 432) and the Chiesa di Sant'Anselmo (home to a pontifical university that includes faculties of theology and philosophy).

🔑 Keyhole Views

Fronting an ornate cypress-shaded piazza, the Roman headquarters of the Sovereign Order of Malta, aka the *Cavalieri di Malta* (Knights of Malta), boasts one of Rome's most celebrated views. It's not immediately apparent, but look through the *buco della serratura* (keyhole) in the villa's green door and you'll see the dome of St Peter's Basilica perfectly aligned at the end of a hedge-lined avenue.

Visit the ornamental piazza (overhauled by the artist and architect Giovanni Battista Piranesi in the late 18th century) and peek through the keyhole either early in the morning or around dinner time to avoid long queues.

Life in the Piazza

THE QUINTESSENTIAL ROMAN LIFESTYLE

Sitting on the steps of a church, taking a refreshing sip of water at a *nasone*, and watching groups of kids kick a ball and old men play cards: it's enchanting to simply let the world go by in a Roman piazza.

RARRARORRO/SHUTTERSTOCK ©

Serenity Amid the Clamour

The feel of an Italian piazza is immediately recognisable: loud, lively and convivial. There's no age limit and no dress code, and you can just be yourself, as relaxed as you are at home. The movement of kids playing a game in front of the church, while senior men gather at their trusty bar, are key to a piazza's ability to make you feel serene and untroubled. The groups of young boys and girls sitting on the steps of the church also contribute to this feeling, as do the visitors consulting their map, and the senior women who've brought their chairs from home to sit and enjoy the gentle breeze before sunset.

These elements are essential for a piazza to work as it should. Rome is blessed with many astounding public squares, but all of them have this common denominator: cosiness.

A Real-Life Movie Set

As summer approaches, Rome has the captivating tendency to become a real-life movie set. The light saturates the orange buildings, making them glow with warmth. A gentle soundtrack of seagull calls and the constant, soothing sound of water in the fountains enhances the magical setting. All these details added to a bustling piazza is like the cherry on the sundae.

Explore tiny alleys and lose yourself in the city centre's cobbled streets, because you may just stumble on your new favourite square. Some piazzas are hidden, some are in plain sight, some are grand and some tiny, but their essence is always the same.

Left Piazza Trilussa **Middle** Piazza della Madonna Dei Monti **Right** Piazza Margana

Essential Ingredients

A Roman piazza has a few indispensable traits: a fountain, a *nasone* (drinking fountain), benches, bars and restaurants, and a sense of harmony and calm, created by a perfect balance between the people and their surroundings. The feel of a piazza can't quite be duplicated anywhere else in the world. Words in Roman dialect are an essential component of the background cacophony, together with klaxons, scooters passing by and (in summer) cicadas.

> Explore tiny alleys and lose yourself in the city centre's cobbled streets, because you may just stumble on your new favourite square.

If you're sitting at a bar with lots of locals around, you'll likely hear the Roman dialect words *'Daje!'* (Come on!) and *'Ao!'* (Hey!) more than *'Ciao!'*. You might also see groups of young people chatting and joking with older people – a heartwarming sight. (A gracious and curious *nonna* might want to chat with you too and tell you about her life.) The secret of all of this is that a multitude of people of different age, social status and religion can meld into one marvellous community, following the formula of the age-old enchantment of Roman piazzas.

☝️ Top Piazzas

Piazza di San Calisto and its bar of the same name offer an excellent introduction to piazza life. **Piazza di San Salvatore in Lauro** offers a more relaxed experience that's enhanced by a glass of wine. **Piazza del Fico** is a party destination popular with young locals. **Piazza Trilussa** is a classic spot to sit and drink on the steps (same for **Piazza della Madonna Dei Monti, Largo dei Librari** and **Piazza Capranica**). For absolute tranquillity, head to **Piazza della Pigna** and **Piazza Margana**, where, at certain times of the day, the only sound you'll hear will be a dog barking or the garbage truck.

34 Traditional Food in TESTACCIO

FOOD | CULTURE | TRADITION

▰▰▰ Testaccio is the most authentic and deeply rooted neighbourhood in the city. Its traditions are well established and its relationship with Roman culinary culture is strong. You can try the best dishes from morning to evening in this part of Rome.

RARRARORO/SHUTTERSTOCK ©

📍 Trip Notes

Getting here Take tram 3.

Neighbourhood hop Take an easy sightseeing walk from Trastevere to Testaccio.

When to go Testaccio is perfect in every season, though restaurants and bars might be closed for holidays in August.

Snacks If you're hungry between stops, go for classic Roman stopgaps *fiori di zucca* (fried zucchini flowers) or *filetto di baccalà* (fried salted cod).

✅ Classic Bites

Pizza rossa (or *bianca* with mortadella), *cacio e pepe* (and carbonara, *amatriciana* and *gricia*) pasta, thin-crust pizza and *supplì* (risotto balls) are the Roman comfort foods par excellence. *Pecorino* cheese, porchetta, spicy *coppiette* (like jerky), and *rosetta* or *ciriola* bread are the best combo for a quick lunch.

TRASTEVERE

Parco Savello

01 Enjoy a slice of *pizza rossa* or warm *pizza bianca* (with perhaps a cookie to follow) at **Panificio Passi**.

05 Pizzeria da Remo a Testaccio has thin-crust Roman pizza and *supplì al telefono* (literally, 'on the phone': the melted mozzarella creates a sort of phone cable).

Ponte Sublicio

Piazza dell'Emporio

Via Querini

Via Gessi

Via Vespucci

Via Vanvitelli

Via Marmorata

02 After a quick lunch of bread, cheese and cured meats at **Salumeria Volpetti**, the perfume of a Roman *alimentari* (deli) will stay with you.

Via Vespucci

Piazza Santa Maria Liberatrice

Via Mastro Giorgio

Via Ginori

Piazza Testaccio

Via Pollione

TESTACCIO

Via Beniamino Franklin

Via Branca

Via Giovanni Battista Bodini

Via Manuzio

Via Ghiberti

Via Volta

Via Galvani

Via Marmorata

03 Mercato di Testaccio offers plenty of choice, from snacks to main dishes.

Parco Monte Testaccio

04 Have dinner at classic trattoria **Felice a Testaccio** (go for the *cacio e pepe* or a meat dish).

Tiber River

SJORS GIJSBERS/SHUTTERSTOCK ©, BOAZ ROTTEM/ ALAMY STOCK PHOTO ©, HAUSER PATRICE/ HEMIS.FR/ALAMY STOCK PHOTO ©

N 0 — 400 m
   0 — 0.2 miles

Listings

BEST OF THE REST

☕ Confectionery & Coffee

Pompi   €
Often packed with locals, Pompi has the best tiramisu in Rome. Don't miss out on the strawberry one.

Charlotte   €
Cookies, macarons, single serves of cheese-cake, chocolate treats and slices of cake are on offer in a delightful setting here.

Caffè Testaccio   €
Buongiorno! Un caffè per favore – dive into Italian culture with a classic coffee break at the counter. No frills, just great coffee.

Caffetteria l'800   €
Between Piazza San Giovanni and the Colosseum, Caffetteria l'800 is great for coffee, homemade tea or a breakfast of tempting *cornetti* (croissants) while sitting outside.

Pasticceria Linari   €
Its delightful pastries and artisanal gelato have made Linari a staple of the *rione* since 1971. Try the traditional *maritozzo* (sweet bun filled with whipped cream) or the *bomboloni* (doughnuts) with cream.

✖ Beautiful Brunches

Sacco Bistrot   €
Brunch in the heart of San Giovanni with a delicious assortment of dishes in an amazing location that was used as a set for Italian movie *The Place*.

Officine San Giovanni   €
San Giovanni is the place to be for brunch, and this industrial-vintage bistrot is a good spot to enjoy it.

I Vitelloni   €
Its decor inspired by Fellini's 1953 film of the same name, I Vitelloni has one of the best brunches in Rome, with an array of savoury and sweet choices. It's open all day.

🏬 Markets to Stroll

Mercato di Via Sannio
Open Monday to Saturday since the '60s, this market sells everything from DVDs, camping equipment, toys and vintage clothes to perfumes.

Mercato di Via Orvieto
The epitome of a *mercato rionale,* Via Orvieto showcases the Roman lifestyle and witty dialect. Here you can buy vegetables, fruit, cheese and meat.

Mercato Metronio (Via Magna Grecia)
Operating since the '50s, this market offers a wonderful selection of Italian produce (vegetables, fruit, dried goods) and regional delicacies (cheese, meat, fish and bakery products) in an atmospheric venue.

Museo delle Mura

🏛 Museums & Walks

Museo delle Mura

At the edge of San Giovanni, this museum in the Porta San Sebastiano has wonderful views of the city and retraces the history of Roman walls and fortifications. It's never crowded.

Fondazione Museo Alberto Sordi

This museum occupies the home of Roman actor Alberto Sordi, who died in 2003. Sordi's films represented the essence of Romans and their city.

Via di San Giovanni in Laterano

Have a drink and enjoy Rome's most colourful street, also known as LGBTIQ St. Its many bars and breathtaking view of the Colosseum make it a perfect spot to linger.

Cimitero Acattolico per gli Stranieri

This cemetery of artists and poets is a must-see amid the chaotic Roman traffic. Cats of the I Gatti della Piramide sanctuary roam freely and greet you as you wander.

🌿 Best of Testaccio

Flavio al Velavevodetto   €€

This restaurant, on the slopes of Monte dei Cocci, has an astonishing setting enhanced by luscious food. It's an institution among locals.

Checchino dal 1887   €€€

Authentic Roman cuisine, rooted in the past and based on the *quinto quarto* (offal), is available here.

PHOTO BETO/GETTY IMAGES ©

Piazza Testaccio

Monte dei Cocci

Monte Testaccio is commonly called Monte dei Cocci (Mt Shards) thanks to the many pieces of broken amphorae from ancient Roman times.

Città dell'Altra Economia

Occupying the huge area of the former Campo Boario (cattle yard and abbatoir), the Città dell'Altra Economia is an interesting place to walk through for a different perspective on Rome. The space now hosts events.

Jumping Wolf

Belgian artist Roa's striking and powerful she-wolf (the animal emblem of Rome), a 30m work on an orange building, is a gift to the neighbourhood and the city.

Piazza Testaccio

Once the headquarters for the local market, this piazza is now the epicentre of neighbourhood life. The Fontana delle Anfore stands right in the middle of it.

SAN GIOVANNI & TESTACCIO REVIEWS

Scan for more things to do in San Giovanni & Testaccio

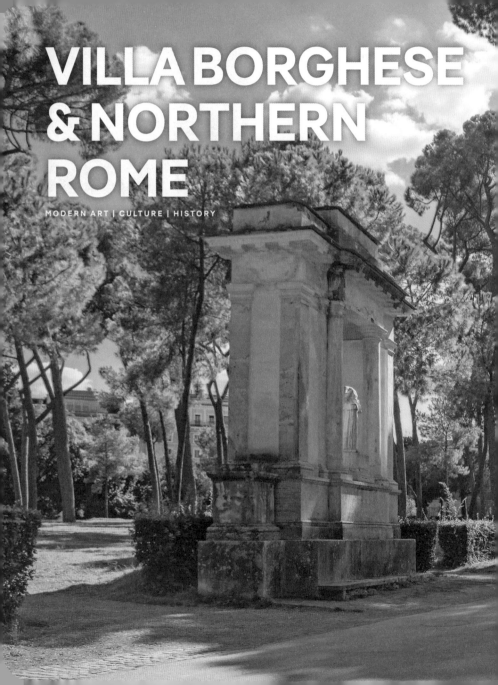

VILLA BORGHESE
& NORTHERN
ROME

MODERN ART | CULTURE | HISTORY

VILLA BORGHESE & NORTHERN ROME
Trip Builder

TAKE YOUR PICK OF MUST-SEES AND HIDDEN GEMS

████████ A mix of ancient and modern history, Villa Borghese and northern Rome offer great eateries, interesting landmarks and relics of Rome's industrial past. Pick any of the lovely parks to unwind in after a day of sightseeing that also takes in Liberty-style (Italian art nouveau) architecture and contemporary art.

🗺 Neighbourhood Notes

Best for Modern architecture, grand villas and great parks

Getting around Explore on foot and hop on any bus to reach further-flung landmarks.

Transport Take the metro to Sant'Agnese–Annibaliano or Bologna.

Tip To avoid crowds, visit the less famous parks on weekends and leave Villa Borghese for a weekday.

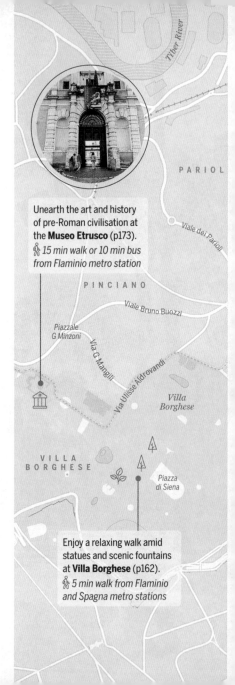

Unearth the art and history of pre-Roman civilisation at the **Museo Etrusco** (p173).
🚶 15 min walk or 10 min bus from Flaminio metro station

PARIOL

Viale dei Parioli

PINCIANO

Viale Bruno Buozzi

Piazzale G Minzoni

Via G Mangili

Via Ulisse Aldrovandi

Villa Borghese

VILLA BORGHESE

Piazza di Siena

Enjoy a relaxing walk amid statues and scenic fountains at **Villa Borghese** (p162).
🚶 5 min walk from Flaminio and Spagna metro stations

Descend to the early-Christian underworld to visit the frescoed **Catacombe di Priscilla** (p168).

🚶 *15 min walk or 10 min bus from Sant'Agnese–Annibaliano metro station*

Villa Ada

T R I E S T E

Go walking or running around **Villa Ada** (p172) one of Rome's largest parks.

🚶 *15 min walk or 10 min bus from Sant'Agnese–Annibaliano metro station*

Explore the catacombs and ancient buildings of the **Basilica di Sant' Agnese** complex (p173).

🚶 *10 min walk from Sant'Agnese–Annibaliano metro station*

S A L A R I O

Discover an unusual Rome with the monsters of Liberty-style **Quartiere Coppedè** (p172).

🚌 *30 min by bus from Termini train station*

N O M E N T A N O

Villa Torlonia

Visit the eclectic Liberty-style buildings of **Villa Torlonia** (p166) urban park.

🚶 *20 min walk or 15 min bus from Sant'Agnese–Annibaliano metro station*

Piazza Salerno

0   500 m
0   0.25 miles

35 Boating at Villa **BORGHESE**

LAKE | PARK | WALKING

▬▬▬ Possibly the most romantic experience you can have in Rome doesn't involve gazing at the skyline from a belvedere. At Villa Borghese you can show off your sailing skills on a boat ride around the gorgeous park. Looking to propose to your better half or rekindle a longstanding love? This is the place to do it.

OBSTO/SHUTTERSTOCK ©

🗺 How to

Getting here Take the metro to Flaminio or Spagna, or a bus (89, 490, 495) or tram (3, 19).

When to go Boats are available year-round, subject to weather.

How much Boat rental is €3 for 20 minutes; admission to Galleria Borghese is €13, to Bioparco zoo €16 (free for children under 1m tall or under 10 years old).

Top prospect Head to the Pincio Terrace for an unparalleled view of Piazza del Popolo.

PAOLO GALLO/SHUTTERSTOCK ©

ARTMEDIAFACTORY/SHUTTERSTOCK ©

Left Galleria Borghese **Far left top** Boating on the lake **Far left bottom** *Apollo and Daphne,* Gian Lorenzo Bernini

On the water This is a must-have romantic experience in the eternal city: hop on a little boat and enjoy the park from a different perspective. You'll get close to the charming corner around the neoclassical Tempio di Esculapio, built by Antonio Asprucci in the late 18th century. Tranquil ducks will keep you company, and you'll be surrounded by beautiful vegetation, including magnolias, purple-flowering paulownias and a Lebanese cedar.

Near the lake Get off the boat and visit the nearby Museo Carlo Bilotti, a permanent exhibition of contemporary art from the Bilotti private collection that includes work by Andy Warhol, Larry Rivers and Giorgio de Chirico. The museum is housed in the Aranciera (Orangery), founded as the residence of the Ceuli noble family. Formerly called the Casino dei Giuochi d'Acqua, the building was used for social events and parties by the powerful Borghese clan from the 18th century and has since undergone many structural changes.

Around the park There are plenty of things to see and do around the fountain-dotted park. Make your way to Galleria Borghese, housed in the 17th-century Villa Borghese mansion and displaying some of the world's most outstanding paintings and sculptures. Kids will love a visit to Bioparco zoo, home to 150 species including reptiles, birds and mammals.

🖼 Galleria Borghese

The superlative collection of artistic compositions at the Galleria Borghese is the result of a ruthless buying campaign launched by Scipione Borghese, nephew of Pope Paul V. By the end of the 17th century the Borghese family boasted 800 paintings and a vast assortment of pieces from Roman antiquity, now part of the Louvre's archaeological collection.

Don't miss *Apollo and Daphne* and *The Rape of Proserpina* by Gian Lorenzo Bernini, Titian's *Sacred and Profane Love*, *The Deposition* by Raphael, Canova's sculpture *Pauline Bonaparte as Venus Victrix*, and Caravaggio's *David with the Head of Goliath* and *Sick Bacchus*.

VILLA BORGHESE
Statues & Fountains

01 Fontana della Venere

In Piazza Scipione Borghese, the 19th-century Venus Fountain consists of a large round basin anchored by a statue of Venus.

02 Fontana dei Cavalli Marini

The four fish-tailed horses in the lower basin of this fountain support an upper basin with their heads.

03 Ferdowsi Statue

Donated by the city of Tehran, this marble statue of the Persian poet who wrote the epic poem 'Shahnameh' was created by Iranian sculptor Sadighi.

04 Goethe Statue

Located in Viale Goethe and donated by German emperor Wilhelm II, this monument to the poet is made of Carrara marble.

05 Lord Byron Statue

This monument to Byron is a marble copy of the original by Bertel Thorvaldsen kept at Trinity College, Cambridge.

06 Victor Hugo Statue

Located in its name-sake piazza, this 1905 statue of the French writer is the work of Lucien Pallez.

07 Umberto I Statue

This bronze equestrian monument to the Italian king in Via della Pineta stands on a porphyry base adorned with bas-reliefs.

08 Tempio di Diana

Near Casina di Raffaello, Asprucci's small 18th-century temple was built in neoclassical style.

09 Tempio di Esculapio

Built by Antonio Asprucci in the 18th century and located in the centre of the lake, this temple is named after the god of medicine.

10 Water Clock

Near the Pincio Hill, this famous and beautiful landmark uses water to move the pendulum.

36

Villa Torlonia Park
PROMENADE

PARK | HISTORY | ARCHITECTURE

▬▬▬▬ An oasis of peace in its park alongside busy Via Nomentana, Villa Torlonia is the youngest of the Roman noble villas. Its intriguing mix of English-style gardens and contemporary mansions creates an impression of wealth and elegance. This little-known oasis has risen from hard times to become a fascinating destination.

VALERIOMEI/SHUTTERSTOCK ©

🗺 How to

Getting here Take the metro to Sant'Agnese–Annibaliano, or a bus (62, 66, 82).

When to go The museums are open Monday to Friday 9am to 7pm. If you'd like to go for a stroll in the park, spring and summer are the best seasons.

How much Admission to Casina delle Civette is €6; with Casino Nobile it's €9.50.

Nearby stops Visit the Sant'Agnese Fuori Le Mura complex, a mix of archaeological ruins and ancient churches.

PHANT/SHUTTERSTOCK ©

CLARA/SHUTTERSTOCK ©

Left Sculptural detail, Saturn Temple **Far left top** Villa Torlonia grounds **Far left bottom** Casina delle Civette

History The estate was founded in 1797 as a country residence for the Pamphilj family. When banker Giovanni Torlonia later bought the villa from the Colonna clan (another powerful Roman clan) he commissioned architect Giuseppe Valadier to turn it into a luxury residence: the Casino Nobile. Between 1925 and 1943 Mussolini rented Casino Nobile, devoting Villa Torlonia to sport and cultural events, and some areas to vegetable plantations and animal farms during WWII.

The park You can go for a walk, have a picnic, do some yoga or just relax in this tidy urban park. There's a lush orchard and exotic vegetation, as well as romantic gardens with a lake. The estate's buildings include the Saturn Temple, neoclassical-style mock-ancient ruins, a tower, two pink-granite obelisks, a beautiful Moorish-style greenhouse, and a Swiss-style cabin that houses the Casina delle Civette museum.

What to do The park itself is small, but it offers an array of entertainment opportunities and noble mansions to explore. The Casino Nobile is home to sculptures and paintings of the Rome School, and Casina delle Civette (named Little House of Owls due to its owl-themed decorations) is a museum of stained glass. Relax with a drink or some lunch at La Limonaia (The Lemon Tree House). Kids can enjoy TechnoTown, a hub for creative science workshops set up by Rome Council.

Villa Torlonia & Mussolini

The peaceful and at times fairy-tale vibe of Villa Torlonia hides a whole underground world, including 2000-year-old Jewish catacombs (unfortunately not accessible to the public) and Mussolini's air-raid shelters.

In 1925 Mussolini moved to Villa Torlonia with his family, paying an annual rent of 1 lira. The family's years here included the wedding of Mussolini's daughter Edda, countless tennis matches, public ceremonies and private parties, but the war inevitably made itself felt.

Between 1940 and 1943, Mussolini built two air-raid shelters and a bunker to protect his family. You can visit the sites with a certified guide: consult en.bunkertorlonia.it.

37 Enter the
CATACOMB

ARCHAEOLOGY | RUINS | FRESCOES

Located in Via Salaria with their entrance facing Villa Ada park, the 35m-deep Catacombe di Priscilla are among the oldest and most beautiful catacombs in Rome. Their ancient and well-preserved frescoes will make this a memorable visit for those who want to unearth a lesser-known side of the city.

How to

Getting here Take the metro to Sant'Agnese–Annibaliano, or a bus (63, 92 or 310).

How much Adult entry costs €8. Book by phone on 06 4542 8493 or email catacombapriscillaseg@gmail.com.

What to wear Choose warm clothing and comfortable shoes.

Nearby stops The Catacombe di Santa Felicita can be visited on request; email protocollo@arcsacra.va or phone 06 446 56 10.

History Priscilla is probably the name of the founder of these early-Christian catacombs or the woman who donated the land where they were built. The cemetery displays a funerary plate devoted to Priscilla, a Roman woman belonging to the family of senators known as gens Acilia. Dug between the 2nd and 5th centuries, the catacombs consist of 13km of tunnels.

Art Head to the upper and central floors for some of the most important archaeological finds. The Cubiculum of the Velatio shows 3rd-century paintings

Above Restored fresco detail, Catacombe di Priscilla **Right top** Nursing mother fresco, Cubiculum of the Velatio **Right bottom** Adoration of the Magi fresco, Greek Chapel

FILIPPO MONTEFORTE/AFP VIA GETTY IMAGES ©

🏛 Catacombs Museum

Complete your tour with a visit to Museo di Priscilla, the Basilica di San Silvestro museum, in the adjacent Villa Ada park. The museum displays fragments of sarcophagi, basic portraits of the deceased, symbolic decorative patterns and classic artwork.

depicting the wedding, maternity and death of the woman buried here. You can see the oldest image of Mary in the Western world in a 3rd-century painting where she is portrayed with the infant Jesus. The unmissable Greek Chapel has 2nd- to 3rd-century frescoes showing biblical episodes such as the Adoration of the Magi and the Resurrection of Lazarus.

Queen of Catacombs The catacombs were known as Regina Catacumbarum because of the large number of martyrs buried here. Among them are the brothers Felix and Philip, likely killed under Diocletian along with their mother, St Felicita. The catacombs host 40,000 graves, including those of at least six popes between the 3rd and 6th centuries.

38 Flaminio REVEALED

WALKING | ART | HISTORY

▰▰▰▰ Boasting modern buildings, eclectic architecture and contemporary art, Flaminio is an elegant and lively neighbourhood that offers an array of great eateries, local markets, and cultural events hosted in cutting-edge exhibition venues. Lovers of theatre and concerts of all types will be in their element and spoilt for choice.

ARCHITECT: RENZO PIANO BUILDING WORKSHOP.
PHOTOGRANK.CH/SHUTTERSTOCK ©

☼ Event Tickets

Book a seat at the Teatro Olimpico (teatroolimpico.it) for dance performances and plays or at the Auditorium Parco della Musica (pictured above; auditorium.com) for concerts featuring Italian and international singers and songwriters playing anything from jazz to pop, as well as dance shows.

🗺 Trip Notes

Getting here Take a bus (53, 168, 910) or tram 2.

Seeing it all You can reach everywhere on foot, but if you're behind schedule, hop on a bus.

When to go There's a lot of ground to cover, so pick a clear day. Avoid summer if you can.

Street-food stop Tuck into a hearty *trapizzino* (stuffed triangular pizza pocket) at the eponymous restaurant near Ponte Milvio.

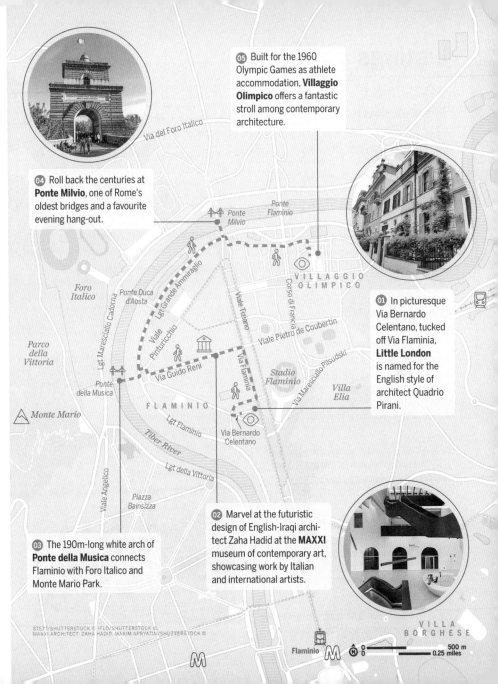

05 Built for the 1960 Olympic Games as athlete accommodation, **Villaggio Olimpico** offers a fantastic stroll among contemporary architecture.

04 Roll back the centuries at **Ponte Milvio**, one of Rome's oldest bridges and a favourite evening hang-out.

01 In picturesque Via Bernardo Celentano, tucked off Via Flaminia, **Little London** is named for the English style of architect Quadrio Pirani.

03 The 190m-long white arch of **Ponte della Musica** connects Flaminio with Foro Italico and Monte Mario Park.

02 Marvel at the futuristic design of English-Iraqi architect Zaha Hadid at the **MAXXI** museum of contemporary art, showcasing work by Italian and international artists.

Via del Foro Italico

Ponte Milvio

Ponte Flaminio

VILLAGGIO OLIMPICO

Foro Italico

Ponte Duca d'Aosta

Viale Grande Ammiraglio

Lgt Maresciallo Cadorna

Viale Pinturicchio

Viale Tiziano

Corso di Francia

Viale Pietro de Coubertin

Via Flaminia

Via Maresciallo Piłsudski

Parco della Vittoria

Ponte della Musica

Via Guido Reni

Stadio Flaminio

Villa Elia

Monte Mario

FLAMINIO

Lgt Flaminio

Tiber River

Via Bernardo Celentano

Lgt della Vittoria

Viale Angelico

Piazza Bainsizza

Flaminio

VILLA BORGHESE

500 m
0.25 miles

VILLA BORGHESE & NORTHERN ROME REVIEWS

Listings

BEST OF THE REST

🍴 Bites & Sweets

Smor €

One-of-a-kind street-food place with the ambitious goal of reproducing recipes from the Viking culinary tradition. It's a feast of smoked fish, rye bread and savoury sauces.

Ops! €€

Teeming with locals, Ops! sets up a daily buffet of entirely plant-based delights, alternating original recipes and its take on traditional dishes from first course to dessert.

Berberè €€

At this cosy place tucked off busy Via Nomentana, the pizza is made with high-quality organic flour and the toppings with locally sourced seasonal ingredients.

Pinsere €

Popular Pinsere serves the oval-shaped Roman *pinsa* (pizza) street-food style. Order your favourite toppings and enjoy your *pinsa* standing at the outdoor shelves or on the go.

Alambicco €€

Open all day, Alambicco welcomes hungry customers with a breakfast of great pastries and coffee drinks, sophisticated dishes for the rest of the day, and a long list of spirits.

Come Il Latte €

Near Porta Pia, one of Rome's best gelaterias guarantees fresh, all-natural gelato and dishes out artisan flavours such as salted caramel, Sicilian pistachio, sour-cherry brittle, and chocolate and cinnamon ricotta.

Momart €€

Close to Piazza Bologna and bursting at the seams with young people is one of the city's trendiest places for an *aperitivo*. For a more formal meal, tuck into delicious pizza or the flavours of traditional cuisine.

Santi Sebastiano e Valentino €€

At this lovely shop the different types of bread (baked daily) are made with high-quality flour blends. It also serves delicious meals from breakfast to dinner.

🚶 Opportunities for Ambling

Villa Ada

Once the residence of the Italian royal family, this English-style garden has neoclassical buildings, a lake and an array of local plants and wildlife, making it a fantastic place to take a break from the city's hustle.

Literary Villa Borghese

Wander through the monumental fountains of Villa Borghese to see all the statues dedicated to writers, including Goethe, Lord Byron and Persian poet Ferdowsi.

Quartiere Coppedè

Built in Liberty style by Italian architect Gino Coppedè, this charming quarter centred

Fontana delle Rane, Quartiere Coppedè

on the Fontana delle Rane (Fountain of the Frogs) in Piazza Mincio will make you feel like you've stepped into a fairy tale: the buildings' facades are decorated with monsters, animals and fairies.

Porta Pia

This majestic gate, designed by Michelangelo, was built between 1561 and 1564. Italian troops breached the Aurelian Walls here to seize Rome from papal rule in 1870.

🖼 Museums, Art & Churches

Sant'Agnese Fuori Le Mura

This important monumental complex off Via Nomentana has catacombs, wonderful mosaics, a 7th-century basilica, the ruins of a 4th-century basilica, and the Mausoleo di St Costanza.

Villa Albani Torlonia

This 18th-century villa in Via Salaria includes large Italian-style gardens, fountains, several buildings and a rich art collection.

Museo Etrusco di Villa Giulia

Here you can explore a fascinating collection of relics and treasures from the Etruscan civilisation, such as the Sarcophagus of the Betrothed found in Cerveteri and a statue of Apollo found in Veio.

Casa del Cinema

Inside Villa Borghese, this complex of three cinemas and an open-air theatre hosts a wide range of cultural events, from book presentations to photography exhibitions to films.

Gigi Proietti Globe Theatre

Located in the heart of Villa Borghese, the timber Elizabethan-style Globe Theatre presents tragedies and comedies by or inspired by William Shakespeare for adults and children.

Museo Etrusco di Villa Giulia

Galleria Nazionale di Arte Moderna e Contemporanea

Next to Villa Borghese, this museum is home to a vast collection of Italian and international art from the 19th to the 21st centuries, housing almost 20,000 pieces.

Explora

At Explora, toys and interactive activities for children between one and eight years old are divided into areas according to age. It's perfect for families. Bookings are mandatory: mdbr.it/en.

MACRO

Located near Porta Pia and built by French architect Odile Decq, MACRO is a new concept of artistic expression, featuring collaboration between different formats including photography and movies.

🛍 Vintage Discoveries

Mercato del Borghetto Flaminio

Peruse the stalls of secondhand dealers to find bargain clothes, vintage homewares and antiques. The market is held in Piazza della Marina every Sunday.

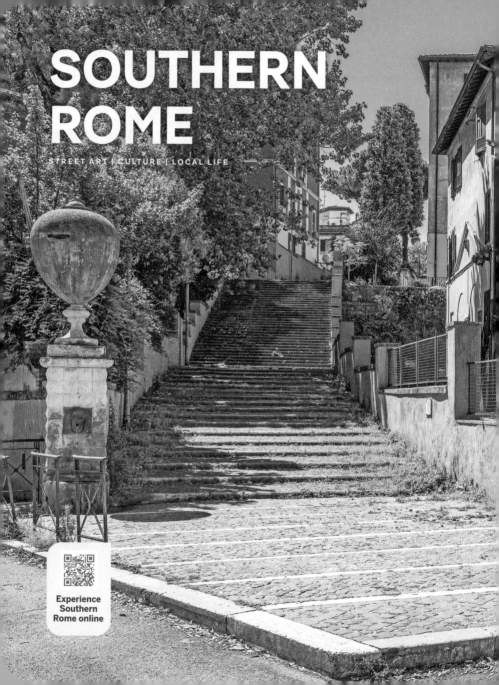

SOUTHERN ROME

STREET ART | CULTURE | LOCAL LIFE

Experience
Southern
Rome online

SOUTHERN ROME
Trip Builder

TAKE YOUR PICK OF MUST-SEES AND HIDDEN GEMS

▬▬▬ The south of Rome is creative, colourful, lively and full of curiosities. From exciting street art to flower-filled courtyards, and from inspiring museums to historical sites immersed in nature, this part of the city has plenty of modern appeal while also keeping tradition alive.

🗺 Neighbourhood Notes

Best for Discovering a new side of the Eternal City

Transport Take the metro to Piramide or Garbatella station.

Getting around The area is very bike friendly thanks to cycle paths and relatively calm streets.

One-of-a-kind neighbourhood The modern architecture in EUR (Esposizione Universale di Roma) will amaze you.

TESTACCIO

Uncover **street art in Ostiense** (p182), starting with Blu's mural at the Aeronautica Militare warehouse.
🚶 *5 min walk from Piramide metro station*

PORTUENSE

Tiber River

Visit the magnificent **Basilica di San Paolo Fuori le Mura** (p190), one of the four Papal Basilicas.
🚶 *5 min walk from San Paolo metro station*

SAN PAOLO

Viale Guido Baccelli

Viale delle Terme di Caracalla

Piazzale Ostiense

Cimitero Acattolico

Piazzale dei Partigiani

Viale Marco Polo

Via Ostiense

OSTIENSE

GARBATELLA

Drop by the **Museo Capitoline Centrale Montemartini** (p190), in a converted thermoelectric power station.
🚶 *10 min walk from Garbatella metro station*

Cycle through 2300 years of history along the **Appia Antica** (p184).
🚌 *15 min by bus 118 from the Colosseum*

Via Ostiense

Piazza Michele da Carbonara

Via Appia Antica

Via Ardeatina

Stroll through the **courtyards of Garbatella** (p186), taking in the neighbourhood's beginnings at Piazza Benedetto Brin.
🚶 *10 min walk from Garbatella metro station*

Via delle Sette Chiese

Via Cristoforo Colombo

Viale Carlo Tommaso Odescalchi

Viale Giustiniano Imperatore

Explore an array of extraordinary street art at the unique **Tor Marancia** complex (p178).
🚶 *30 min walk from Marconi metro station*

N
0   500 m
0   0.25 miles

39 Tor Marancia's Artistic
BONANZA

WALKS | STREET ART | CULTURE

▬▬▬ Southern Rome has the world's first open-air museum of street art. Explore beyond the centre to discover a complex of buildings that gives you free access to more than 20 giant masterpieces and offers a new perspective on this art-loving city.

DIAMOND ©

🗺 How to

Getting here From Piramide take bus 716 to the Caravaggio/Tor Marancia stop.

When to go The museum (Via di Tor Marancia 63) is open 24 hours, but it's best to visit in the daytime so you can admire the pieces in natural light.

From Ostiense Tor Marancia is fairly close to the Ostiense neighbourhood and can be reached by bike or on foot from there.

Beyond the art As you explore, notice the details of daily life, such as colourful balconies and windows.

EDUCATION IMAGES/GETTY IMAGES ©

GENNARO LEONARDO/GETTY IMAGES ©

Left & Far left bottom Big City Life murals, Tor Marancia **Far left top** *Hic Sunt Adamantes,* Diamond

Big City Life This is the official name of the project that began in 2015 when artists donated their work to enliven a little-visited part of Rome.

Highlights *Il Bambino Redentore* by Seth, depicting a child on a ladder, is one of the most popular works, exuding a sense of hope and innocence. Jericho's wonderful *Distanza Uomo Natura* represents the bond between humans and the natural world. *Hic Sunt Adamantes* by Italian artist Diamond evokes a Rome that is eager to change and wake up, personified by a sleepy woman with a diamond in her hand. *Il Ponentino* by Pantonio is a visionary representation of the famous Roman breeze called the Ponentino. *Alme Sol Invictus* by Domenico Romeo symbolises the sun and expresses a hope for the rebirth and renewal of the neighbourhood.

Shanghai connection Don't miss the *Nostra Signora di Shanghai* by Roman artist Mr Klevra, portraying a breathtaking Virgin Mary. The wall where this work is painted was blessed with holy water by the pastor of the local church. Visible outside the complex, *Welcome to Shanghai* by Caratoes portrays a traditional Chinese figure holding an origami depiction of the she-wolf, symbol of Rome, to show the kinship between Rome and Shanghai.

ⓘ The Shanghai Nickname

Tor Marancia acquired the nickname 'Shanghai' after 1933, when the area's population density dramatically increased after many people were thrown out of their houses in central Rome during the fascist regime. Frequent floods once hit this area of former marshland, which also made it reminiscent of Shanghai.

Though the nickname's origins aren't particularly flattering to Shanghai, Tor Marancia is very proud of its moniker, as the numerous street-art references to the Chinese city make plain. Just as Shanghai has grown into a mighty metropolis, locals feel their neighbourhood has overcome its uncertain beginnings and developed into a wonderful part of modern Rome.

The Cats of Rome

**THE FELINE
ROMAN EMPIRE**

For centuries cats have been beloved residents of the Eternal City, and there are countless stories, legends and curious facts about them. Cats are real citizens of Rome and they've always played an important part in the city's identity.

SOPHIE LENOIR/SHUTTERSTOCK ©

Paws on cobblestones and twitching tails peeking around the corner of a pastel-orange alley: cats are unequivocally a feature of Rome, and well they know it. Throughout the city, elderly women commonly known as *gattare* (cat ladies) proudly take care of them, and cats are engraved in the architecture and surroundings. There are many popular tales and hidden details about the city's feline residents, past and present.

Local legends There are several stories to explain the significance of the little statue of a cat that you'll see if you look up in Via della Gatta. One says that it commemorates a cat that was meowing loudly to draw attention to a child about to fall from the spot where the statue now stands. A second story is similar but says the cat was meowing to warn of a night-time fire in the street that was slowly getting out of hand. A third story has it that the cat is looking in the direction of hidden treasure.

It's said that Piazza Sallustio was once a real haven for cats, who'd eat restaurant leftovers there – particularly on Fridays, when in Rome it's typical to eat fish.

Emperor Augustus wrote verses to his cat, declaring her 'the most intimate friend of my old age'.

In ancient Rome, some guards were commonly called *catti* (which resembles the modern Italian word for cats, *gatti*) because they needed to have sharp eyes at night-time, like a cat.

Cat-loving poets, writers and actors Plenty of Roman poets, such as Gioacchino Belli and Trilussa (statues of both can be found in the Trastevere neighbourhood),

Left Residents of Largo Argentina
Middle Via della Gatta street sign
Right Cimitero Acattolico per gli Stranieri

made cats living in Rome one of the muses for their poetry. Roman actors such as Anna Magnani and writers such as Alberto Moravia have a deep and strong relationship with cats.

Famous cats of Rome The Italian version of animated film *The Aristocats* has a protagonist called Romeo – and in Italian 'Romeo' rhymes with 'Colosseo'. A locally cherished line from one of the film's songs goes: 'Romeo, er mejo der Colosseo' (Romeo, the best of the Colosseum) – that is, the best cat in Rome.

> Cats are unequivocally a feature of Rome, and well they know it. Throughout the city, elderly women proudly take care of them, and cats are engraved in the architecture.

Pupone was one of the most famous cats in Trastevere. Sadly, he passed away in 2009, but if you walk along Vicolo del Leopardo you'll find a shrine dedicated to him.

At Largo Argentina, Rome's best-known cat sanctuary, you have the chance to meet Trudeau, an extra-friendly fluffy black cat who likes to saunter as if he's the king of Rome.

Give in to cats' charming ways and be entranced by one of the biggest and most beautiful love stories you can witness between a city and its animal residents.

Where to Spot Roman Cats

Cats are easily found as you stroll around the city, but there are a few particular places where you can admire them in all their freedom and beauty. Start at Vicolo del Leopardo in Trastevere, then move along to the hidden cat sanctuary in Piazza Vittorio and then the biggest sanctuary in the city in Largo Argentina. More cats can be found at the many feline oases around Rome, like the one near Porta Portese market; in Piramide inside the Cimitero Acattolico per gli Stranieri; and at the Cimitero di Campo Verano, close to San Lorenzo.

40 Spy Street Art in OSTIENSE

ART | CULTURE | ARCHITECTURE

■■■■ Once a Roman industrial hub, Ostiense still has an incomparable urban charm. From its roads to its imposing and jaw-dropping street art, this neighbourhood is the heart of a Rome few visitors see. Wander the neighbourhood to discover the most colourful streets in the city and take in some wonderful art.

🗺 How to

Getting here Take the metro to Piramide.

When to go Go in daytime to see the artwork. An evening visit allows you to sample the area's famous nightlife.

Getting around The neighbourhood is highly walkable and wonderfully bike friendly.

Bonus art Look out for sticker art on traffic signs, walls and letterboxes.

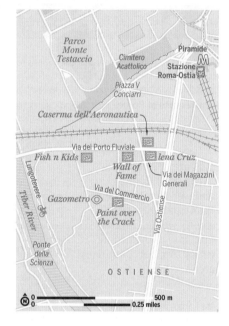

The aesthetic of Ostiense is truly unusual. Amid wondrous thousand-year-old fragments that still stand and amaze, this neighbourhood reveals another seductive aspect of Roman history. A 1900s industrial complex peeking through quintessentially Roman buildings is the star attraction, together with some sensational street art.

The artist Blu has covered two facades of the Caserma dell'Aeronautica (the former Aeronautica Militare warehouse) with different colourful faces, each telling a specific story enriched by the history and visual

Right top *Hunting Pollution,* Iena Cruz **Right bottom** *Fish 'n Kids,* Agostino Iacurci

☀ Summer Events & Cycling

Walk along Via del Commercio to see the Gazometro, a massive cylindrical structure that's a local landmark – it hosts events throughout summer. Go down the stairs right after the Ponte della Scienza to ride along the Lungotevere cycle path.

references that characterise the area. Iena Cruz has created Europe's biggest ecological artwork to adorn a building: the paint eats smog, transforming it into harmless dust. *Fish 'n Kids* by Agostino Iacurci illustrates a man happily swimming with fish to convey the dream of nature and humankind peacefully coexisting.

Further on, the centrepiece of Ostiense street art is *Wall of Fame* by JB Rock, where superstars of every kind appear one after another over a long distance. *Paint over the Crack* by London-based artist Kid Acne is the perfect location for a post-industrial shot of Rome.

Keep an eye out for tags and smaller artworks as you stroll: art is absolutely everywhere.

41 Cycle the Appia ANTICA

NATURE | HISTORY | SPORT

Breathtaking countryside right in the heart of the city: welcome to the extraordinary Appia Antica cycle path. Alongside mausoleums and villas, atop aqueducts running through fields, and past sheep and horses, the path takes you through 2300 years of history. Discover the oldest highway in the world.

SUN_SHINE/SHUTTERSTOCK ©

🗺 Trip Notes

Getting here Rent a bike in the city, then ride down Via di Porta San Sebastiano. The path begins around 20 minutes' ride from the centre.

When to go Spring or autumn are the most enjoyable seasons.

Sheep in the city In Parco della Caffarella, look out for the shepherd with his sheep. The animals roam freely and it's such a fun scene to witness.

🚲 Cycling Tips

Due to the bumpy path, the use of a mountain bike is highly recommended. If riding in the summer, rent an electric bike to make your excursion more comfortable. Take a break at Bar Cecilia Metella, with its hidden garden, where kind Roman ladies will greet you with a smile.

Rik Velner,
bike tour expert

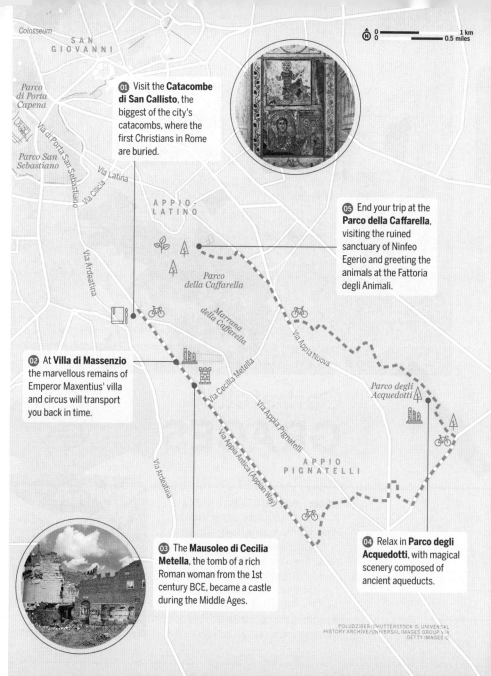

Colosseum

SAN GIOVANNI

Parco di Porta Capena

Parco San Sebastiano

Via di Porta San Sebastiano

Via Latina

Via Cilicia

APPIO LATINO

Via Ardeatina

Parco della Caffarella

Merrana della Caffarella

Via Cecilia Metella

Via Appia Nuova

Via Appia Pignatelli

Via Ardeatina

Via Appia Antica (Appian Way)

APPIO PIGNATELLI

Parco degli Acquedotti

01 Visit the **Catacombe di San Callisto**, the biggest of the city's catacombs, where the first Christians in Rome are buried.

05 End your trip at the **Parco della Caffarella**, visiting the ruined sanctuary of Ninfeo Egerio and greeting the animals at the Fattoria degli Animali.

02 At **Villa di Massenzio** the marvellous remains of Emperor Maxentius' villa and circus will transport you back in time.

03 The **Mausoleo di Cecilia Metella**, the tomb of a rich Roman woman from the 1st century BCE, became a castle during the Middle Ages.

04 Relax in **Parco degli Acquedotti**, with magical scenery composed of ancient aqueducts.

0 1 km
0 0.5 miles

42 Garbatella GRACES

GARDENS | CULTURE | LIFESTYLE

████ Imagine a village within a city, where locals enjoy their shared courtyards, have dinner with their neighbours and hang their laundry in communal drying racks, all while surrounded by typical 1920s Roman architecture and the labyrinthine beauty of neighbourhood gardens. This village's name is Garbatella.

🗺️ How to

Getting here Ride the metro to Garbatella station, or you could take a 20-minute walk from the Ostiense neighbourhood.

Church view The dome you might see peeking through the buildings belongs to the Chiesa di San Francesco Saverio.

When to go Garbatella is a joy in any season. Visit on a Sunday, when everything is quieter than usual, or on a weekday morning for a glimpse of daily life.

A Delightful Maze

Garbatella is one of the most Roman neighbourhoods in the city thanks to its vibe, local traditions and undeniable beauty. The atmosphere is like that of a small country village: just about everybody knows each other, and everything feels accessible, unpretentious and instantly homey. This area has a particular characteristic that can't be found anywhere else in the city: the number of courtyards and green spaces. Garbatella was built as a *città giardino* (garden city), where people, nature and modernity could live in harmony, and it has succeeded wonderfully at this.

The streets and alleys of Garbatella are like a delightful maze to get lost in, and that is the perfect way to discover this part of the

📷 Must-See Spots

Be sure to pass by the **Fontana di Carlotta**, a little fountain said to represent the *ostessa* from whom Garbatella takes its name; **Piazza Benedetto Brin**, with the neighbourhood's first buildings; and the 1920s **Teatro Palladium**.

Left Garbatella courtyard
Above left Bar dei Cesaroni (p189)
Above right Fontana di Carlotta

city. A few gates might be closed, but most of them are open and ready to be entered. Don't be afraid to come in and look around: if a gate is open (and there's no sign forbidding entry), you're allowed in. Always greet people as you encounter them – locals are happy and proud to see visitors appreciating their charming neighbourhood.

Locals & Lifestyle

As you greet the locals, you might even start a pleasant chat and ask all about the neigh-bourhood. A great place for this is at the bar in front of the church, where plenty of elderly men can be found playing cards and drinking coffee or *grappa*. Nobody knows better than a *nonno* or a *nonna*.

Laundry is also another fascinating trait of this area: communal clotheslines are placed in the middle of courtyards. The colours and textures of bed linen and tablecloths are the perfect backdrop to your walk around Garbatella.

🖼 Street-Art Break

Rome loves street art, and even a traditional area such as Garbatella loves the breath of fresh air talented artists bring with them – especially when their muse is the neighbourhood itself.

In Via Passino, close to Piazza Damiano Sauli, just around the corner, you can admire *Oh My Darling Clementine* by Solo and Diamond. It's a huge and wonderful portrait of the woman from whom Garbatella is said to have taken its name.

The walls of CSOA La Strada are covered to the roof in artworks inspired by notable political events, both historical and contemporary.

Left Street murals, Garbatella **Below** Votive street altar, Garbatella

Sport, Cinema & TV

The neighbourhood's relationship to Roman culture is immediately visible. You'll see the Roma football-club flag and logo almost everywhere – look out for a minimal portrait of a she-wolf with its mouth open.

Murals dedicated to famous figures are commonly seen. There are images of famous Italian actor Alberto Sordi in Via Persico *and* Via Rubino.

A relatively modern point of interest in Garbatella is the colourful and authentic Bar dei Cesaroni, location of Roman TV series *I Cesaroni*.

Local Legend

There's no official history of the name Garbatella, but there are plenty of tales. The best known relates to an *ostessa* (hostess of an *osteria*, a typical Roman restaurant) who was considered to be *garbata e bella* (kind and beautiful). The two words run together to make 'Garbatella'.

Listings

BEST OF THE REST

Museums & Architecture

Ponte Settimia Spizzichino

This imposing white bridge with an unusual shape is a feature of the daily commute for many locals. Built in 2009, it has became another landmark of the area.

Centrale Montemartini

Once a thermoelectric power station, the unique Centrale Montemartini is now a museum housing ancient pieces. It's the second exhibition space of the Capitoline Museum.

Polo Museale ATAC

Trains, trams and the story of ATAC (Rome's transportation system): you can learn about it all here, with old wagons and carriages that you can walk into. Find it inside Piramide metro station.

Basilica di San Paolo Fuori le Mura

Part of the four Papal Basilicas and the second biggest after St Peter's – this is a mandatory stop to admire one of the most beautiful churches outside the Aurelian Walls.

Breakfasts for Champions

Bar dei Cesaroni   €

This place has the classic atmosphere you need for a proper Roman breakfast. Enjoy your coffee, *cornetto* (croissant) and newspaper while sitting outside, but don't forget to check out the interior: Roman decor at its best.

Marigold   €€

Healthy, fresh and produced with care, the natural and delicious breakfast at Marigold is rich in flavour. There are pastries, eggs, avocado on toast and locally brewed coffee for your morning needs.

Bar Moriconi   €

In need of an authentic Roman bar? Moriconi is your go-to destination. Locals and even cats love to stop by this cosy vintage spot.

Pasticceria Walter Musco   €€

Artisanal gelato, high-quality pastries and a wide selection of interesting desserts, from small bites to whole cakes, are on offer here. Choose a sweet treat to go with your excellent coffee.

Andreotti   €

In business since 1931, and recognised as a 'historical shop', Andreotti is a great spot for coffee, breakfast, gelato or a snack. To qualify as a historical shop, a business must have been in the hands of three generations of the same family and open for at least 70 years.

Aperitivo, Cocktails & Bistrot

Romeow Cat Bistrot   €€

Having breakfast, lunch or dinner in the company of playful, charming cats is a perk of the area. At this cat cafe the menu is entirely vegan and simply delicious.

Ponte Settimia Spizzichino

Doppiozeroo €

A few steps from the Gazometro, this cool spot offers wine, bubbles and a tasty selection of salty bites (such as pasta and pizza). It's the perfect pre-dinner stop.

Latteria Garbatella €€

With a delightful ambience, this place has one of the best terraces for enjoying a round of cocktails prepared with intriguing and luscious ingredients.

Angeli Rock €

An institution, Angeli Rock is excellent for a tasty *aperitivo* while watching a sunset from the terrace. It offers seriously good food and drinks.

Tre de Tutto €

Right at the beautiful entrance to Garbatella, this cute and unpretentious spot is perfect for a cocktail or *aperitivo*. Immerse yourself in an authentic Roman setting here.

 **Market Discoveries**

Mercatino Garbatella

Hunt through this place to find your treasure. There's everything from trinkets to fancy books to furniture, plus a great selection of local art, Italian culture magazines and one-of-a-kind items.

Ex Novo

Ex Novo has an overflowing and fun mix of unexpected secondhand objects, from clothing to furniture, plus books, collectables, DVDs, records and homewares.

Farmers Market San Paolo

This farmers market has fresh regional produce and a huge variety of wine, oil, cheese and more to choose from. Venture south of the city on a weekend day to browse your options.

SIBIL PHOTOS/SHUTTERSTOCK ©

Centrale Montemartini

 Bread-Based Delights

Forno Angeli €

Cookies, pizza and bread are on offer in this family-style traditional shop. It's perfect for a midday snack or quick lunch, or for stocking up on delicious biscuits to bring home.

Elettroforno Frontoni €

Enjoy pizza by the slice in infinite flavours (*mortadella* and *burrata* or *pizza bianca* with tasty seasonal fillings) and the crunchiest, tastiest bread.

Il Forno Antico di Roma €

This place is fully in the 'locals only' area, but if you do get here you'll be able to taste some of the best *pizza rossa* in Rome: well sauced and incredibly rich in taste.

La Fornarina dal 1989 €

At this local bakery, tradition, love and good ingredients combine to create a range of excellent salty and sweet options, from fragrant bread to regional cookies.

 Scan for more things to do in Southern Rome

SOUTHERN ROME REVIEWS

DAY TRIPS

LAKES | VILLAGES | SEA

DAY TRIPS
Trip Builder

TAKE YOUR PICK OF MUST-SEES AND HIDDEN GEMS

Rome is part of the glorious region of Lazio, home to a wealth of enchanting destinations. Whether it's food and wine, local history or the great outdoors you love, it's all there, just a short drive or train ride away. Dive right in, living and breathing the region like a local.

🗺️ Trip Notes

Best for Stunning hidden history and authentic local life

Transport and getting around Car is the best option, but towns in the region are easily reached by train from Termini.

Challenge your palate Try the local specialities suggested by restaurant hosts and explore the region's fresh farm-to-table produce.

Discover five of the most delightful towns in Lazio, beginning with **Civita di Bagnoregio** (p203).
🚗 *30 min drive from Viterbo Porta Romana station*

Lago di Bolsena

● Civitavecchia

Mediterranean Sea

0 — 40 km
0 — 20 miles

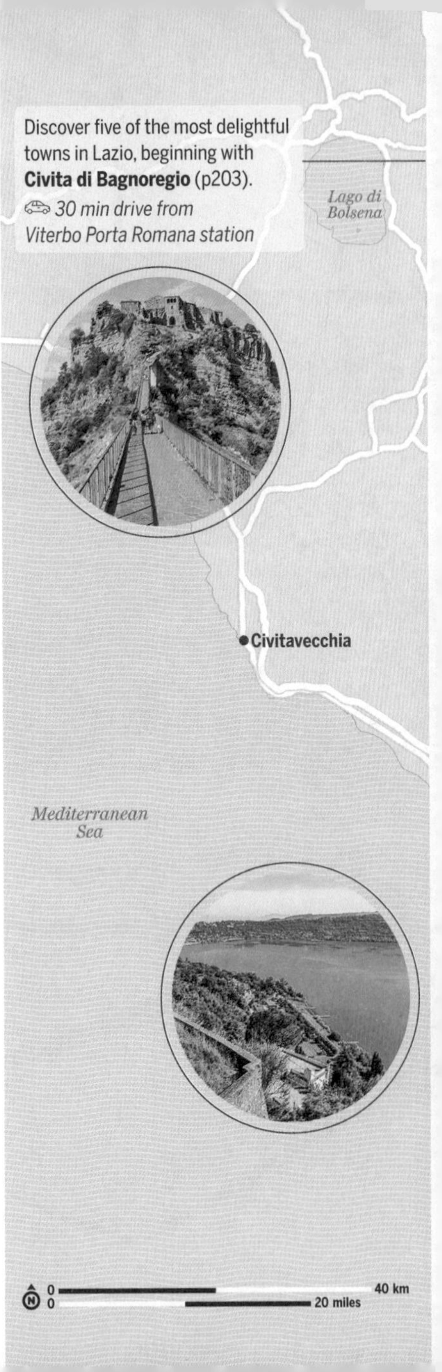

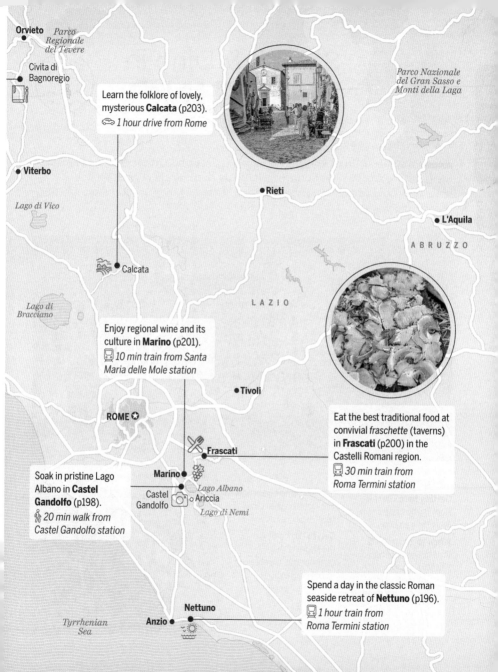

Orvieto

Parco Regionale del Tevere

Civita di Bagnoregio

Learn the folklore of lovely, mysterious **Calcata** (p203).
🚗 *1 hour drive from Rome*

Parco Nazionale del Gran Sasso e Monti della Laga

Viterbo

Rieti

Lago di Vico

L'Aquila

ABRUZZO

Lago di Bracciano

Calcata

LAZIO

Enjoy regional wine and its culture in **Marino** (p201).
🚆 *10 min train from Santa Maria delle Mole station*

Tivoli

ROME ✪

Eat the best traditional food at convivial *fraschette* (taverns) in **Frascati** (p200) in the Castelli Romani region.
🚆 *30 min train from Roma Termini station*

Frascati

Marino

Soak in pristine Lago Albano in **Castel Gandolfo** (p198).
🧍 *20 min walk from Castel Gandolfo station*

Castel Gandolfo

Lago Albano
Ariccia
Lago di Nemi

Spend a day in the classic Roman seaside retreat of **Nettuno** (p196).
🚆 *1 hour train from Roma Termini station*

Nettuno

Tyrrhenian Sea

Anzio

43 Splash & Dine in NETTUNO

SEA | CULTURE | FOOD

■■■ In summer, do as Romans do: take a train, or hop in your car, and escape the heat by going straight to the beach. Pretty Nettuno offers great food, a sense of history and an attractive maritime lifestyle. Enjoy its local atmosphere, sounds and views.

🗺 How to

Getting here The train from Termini takes a bit more than an hour.

When to go The ideal time to visit is between late May and mid-September, though Lazio's summery weather

means you might be able to enjoy some beach time into October, when the sea is less crowded.

Gelato Walk along the shore with a scrumptious ice cream from Le Streghe.

Left Piazza Marcantonio Colonna
Far left top Nettuno Beach Far left
bottom Local seafood pasta

Nettuno is a little jewel that offers more than meets the eye:

Beach-time essentials In bathing suit and flip-flops, with a newspaper tucked under their arm, *Nettunesi* are immediately recognisable. The feel of the place is encapsulated by the unmistakable sound of vintage wooden clogs paired with voices perfectly synched to the waves. Be sure to buy a slice of *pizza bianca* (the official midmorning snack when you're at the Roman seaside) at a local bakery and a crossword magazine at a newspaper kiosk before you rent your *ombrellone* (parasol) and *sdraio* (chairs). Nettuno has many beautiful free beaches.

Medieval borgo Life here revolves around the enchanting little medieval hamlet. At lunch or dinner, venture from the beach for an appetising plate of seafood pasta. Cute little alleys that will make you think of Trastevere will lead you to Romolo al Borgo, one of the best restaurants in Nettuno, with tables outside in the main piazza. Enjoy its true Italian vibe while you dine on some of the best fish-based dishes you'll ever taste. Caffè Volpi and the main bar on Piazza Marcantonio Colonna are two great spots for a classic *caffè* or *aperitivo*. Go with the first for the local atmosphere and with the second for its pretty view over the harbour.

Sights & Beach Clubs

Visit Forte Sangallo, built in 1501 to defend the city from sea storms, and explore Nettuno's history at the museum, which houses a collection of local archeological finds. The Santuario di Santa Maria Goretti is the town's main religious and architectural symbol, and the 20-storey-high Hotel Scacciapensieri punctuates the *Nettunese* skyline. Fontana del Nettuno bubbles away in Piazza Mazzini.

Nettuno offers a fine selection of beach clubs where you can rent your parasol and chairs for a day or more. Try Bagni Pro Loco, Bagni Belvedere or Stabilimento Tirrenino.

Relax Lakeside in Castel
GANDOLFO

LAKE | FOOD | LIFESTYLE

▬▬▬ Surrounded by wonderful views, Castel Gandolfo offers the best take on lakeside life while also being strongly tied to regional traditions. Swim, eat and stroll to your heart's content in this magical place.

ESSEVU/SHUTTERSTOCK ©

🗺 How to

Getting here Take the train from Termini, direction Albano Laziale, and get out at Castel Gandolfo. The ticket is only a couple of euros and the ride takes about half an hour.

When to go Go in spring for pleasant walks in mild temperatures and in summer for a refreshing day of lake swimming.

Tip Visit on the weekend if you plan to see the Palazzo Pontificio.

SOPOTNICKI/SHUTTERSTOCK ©

LUCA LORENZELLI/SHUTTERSTOCK ©

Left Palazzo Pontificio **Far left top** Lago Albano views **Far left bottom** Streetside cafes

Castel Gandolfo is a slice of paradise with its pristine lake (once a volcano!), restaurants along the shore and enchanting *borgo* (medieval village).

Stroll through the borgo When you arrive, brace yourself for a steep walk towards the top of the town. It may take a while, and it could be a bit tiring, but once you're there the stunning medieval village will be well worth the effort. There are little shops and bars to lose yourself in, and a feeling of easy living will envelop you. Wander around to discover panoramic views of Lago Albano.

Swim in the lake Cool off with a dive into the beautiful lake – the long shoreline offers plenty of options. You can rent a parasol and chairs, or just sit on the rocks with your feet dangling in the water and greet the friendly ducks passing by. Locals windsurf and canoe here. If you'd like to join them, contact Canoa Kayak Academy (ckacademy.it/en/tours/kayak-rental).

Local dishes From classic Roman pasta dishes to lesser-known local culinary traditions, restaurants here love to celebrate the town's culture. Try the huge, tempting antipasto at Da Agnese trattoria, right at the water's edge and with one of the most beautiful outlooks. Be sure to try the speciality of Castel Gandolfo: *pesche al vino* (peaches in white wine).

🏛 Standout Sights

Piazza della Libertà is the heart of the *borgo*. Drink an espresso at Bar Carosi, where you can do some people-watching and admire the stunning Chiesa di San Tommaso da Villanova, designed by Bernini.

The Palazzo Pontificio, the Pope's summer residence, is another must-see. Its wondrous gardens are the equal of those at Villa Cybo and Villa Barberini.

If you're travelling by car, make a side trip to the outstanding Abbazia Greca di San Nilo, founded in 1004. About 20 minutes' drive from Castel Gandolfo, the abbey is the only surviving Italo-Greek monastery.

45 Fraschette
FLAVOURS

FOOD | TRADITIONS | CULTURE

▬▬▬ Cheese, cold cuts, bread, pasta and salty bites paired with the best wines of the Castelli Romani area – the *fraschetta* isn't just a place; it's a tradition. A meal here exemplifies the classic Roman combination of conviviality and food culture.

🗺️ How to

Getting here Car is best, but you can also travel by train from Termini – just be ready to walk or cycle a bit.

When to go *Fraschette* are traditional for Sunday lunch, but you can visit any time (confirm that places will be open).

Bike travel Pay a supplement and bring your bike on the train.

The essence of the Castelli Romani can be summed up as living simply, eating well and drinking good wine. The area particularly excels at the latter, with wines ranging from Cannellino di Frascati DOCG to the typical *fraschetta* drop called Romanella, a light, sweet, sparkling wine that's perfect with salty food.

In Frascati, Osteria Fraschetta Trinca offers a selection of regional cheeses (*pecorino*) and cold cuts (mortadella, porchetta), plus the classic *ciambelline al vino*

Right top Frascati wines **Right bottom** Deli items, Ariccia

ⓘ Fraschetta ABC

The beauty of the *fraschette* is how inexpensive and high-quality they are at the same time. Don't worry if something seems way too cheap, because that's how the tradition works. Order a carafe of house wine and a platter with all the specialities, then sit back and savour.

(doughnut-shaped cookies made with wine), all in a very informal setting.

The official wine town in Lazio is Marino, which hosts the Sagra dell'Uva (Grape Festival) every October. In 2016 the town's fountains were running with red wine instead of water! Eat at Il Fratone to enjoy a family-style meal of traditional Roman specialities such as *pollo con peperoni* (chicken with bell peppers) or *cotiche con fagioli* (pork crackling with beans).

Convivial Ariccia, with an appealingly light and fun atmosphere, is another favourite stop for lunching Romans. Stop at wonderfully secluded La Selvotta, where porchetta and wine are served on classic long wooden tables surrounded by century-old chestnut trees. For a quick snack, enjoy a platter of regional cheeses and meats at Chiosco Pepparone.

46 Five Villages ROAD TRIP

HISTORY | LIFESTYLE | CULTURE

▬▬▬ Every region in Italy has an array of wonderful little towns and villages that are completely unknown – often even to people elsewhere in the region. Lazio is full of these gorgeous *borghi*, especially in Viterbo, province of history, culture and tradition. Tour five of the most beautiful and lesser-known villages for a one-of-a-kind experience.

🗺 Trip Notes

Getting here Start early to begin your itinerary with the best light and allow yourself to take your time throughout the day.

When to go Autumn (particularly September) is best, when the weather is flawless and places aren't too crowded. Avoid weekends in summer.

Be prepared Bring plenty of water, and wear comfortable shoes (villages tend to have rough paths and steep climbs).

🌿 Bonus Breaks

This route is packed with wonderful additional stops, such as the Parco Regionale Valle del Treja, a green paradise to trek; Lago di Monterosi, a hidden oasis; and the Sacro Bosco di Bomarzo, a monumental complex embedded in a park and adorned by sculptures of monsters and mythological figures.

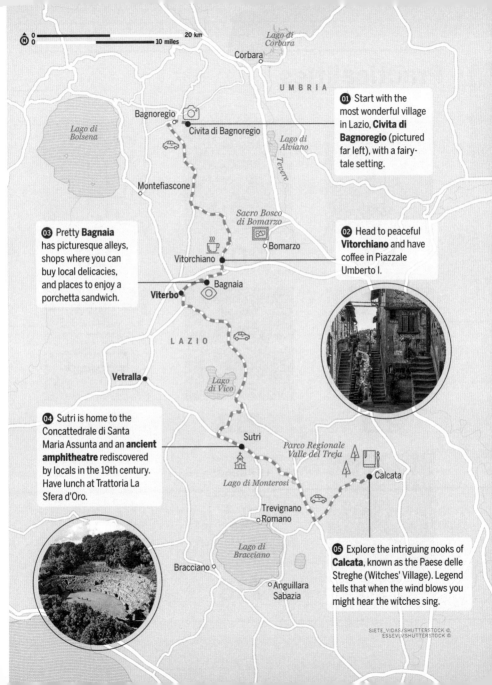

01 Start with the most wonderful village in Lazio, **Civita di Bagnoregio** (pictured far left), with a fairy-tale setting.

03 Pretty **Bagnaia** has picturesque alleys, shops where you can buy local delicacies, and places to enjoy a porchetta sandwich.

02 Head to peaceful **Vitorchiano** and have coffee in Piazzale Umberto I.

04 Sutri is home to the Concattedrale di Santa Maria Assunta and an **ancient amphitheatre** rediscovered by locals in the 19th century. Have lunch at Trattoria La Sfera d'Oro.

05 Explore the intriguing nooks of **Calcata**, known as the Paese delle Streghe (Witches' Village). Legend tells that when the wind blows you might hear the witches sing.

Lago di Corbara

Corbara

UMBRIA

Bagnoregio

Civita di Bagnoregio

Lago di Bolsena

Lago di Alviano

Montefiascone

Tevere

Sacro Bosco di Bomarzo

Bomarzo

Vitorchiano

Bagnaia

Viterbo

LAZIO

Vetralla

Lago di Vico

Sutri

Parco Regionale Valle del Treja

Calcata

Lago di Monterosi

Trevignano Romano

Lago di Bracciano

Bracciano

Anguillara Sabazia

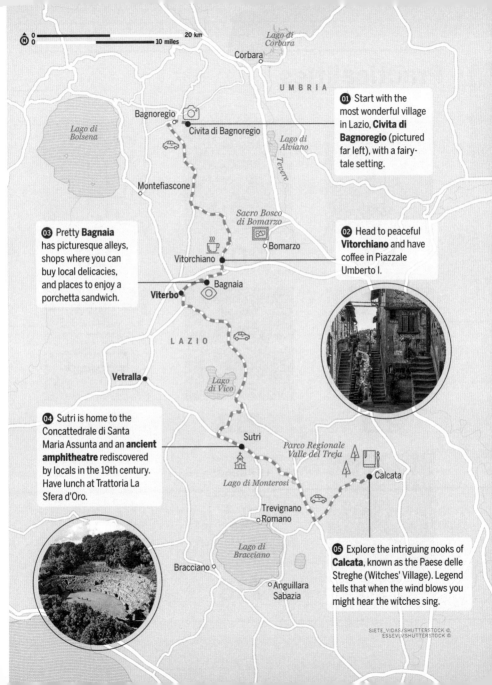

SIETE_VIDAS/SHUTTERSTOCK ©, ESSEVU/SHUTTERSTOCK ©

20 km

10 miles

Practicalities

ARRIVING

206

GETTING AROUND

208

SAFE TRAVEL

210

MONEY

211

RESPONSIBLE TRAVEL

212

ACCOMMODATION

214

ESSENTIALS

216

LANGUAGE

218

Right Piazza Navona (p64)

EASY STEPS FROM THE AIRPORT TO THE CITY CENTRE

Rome has two international airports – Fiumicino (FCA) and Ciampino (CIA) – and neither of them is actually in Rome. With 40 million passengers annually, Fiumicino (Leonardo da Vinci) Airport is Rome's main transport hub, and despite being further from the city (30km west) features much better connections. The smaller Ciampino Airport, 15km south of the centre, is used mostly by low-cost airlines.

AT THE AIRPORT

SIM CARDS
Vodafone and TIM sell SIM cards for unlocked phones in Terminal 3 of Fiumicino Airport, although prepaid prices tend to be much higher than in the city. You will need ID to purchase a SIM card in Italy.

CURRENCY EXCHANGE
There are exchange services in the departure and arrival terminals of Fiumicino and Ciampino airports. Rates aren't great; exchange in the city if possible.

WI-FI Free wi-fi is provided in both airports. To connect, select the Airport Free Wifi network and you'll be redirected to a welcome page in the language your phone is set to.

ATMS Both Fiumicino and Ciampino have ATMs, but exchange rates are far from favourable.

EATING Most places to eat in Fiumicino Airport are located in Terminal 3, by boarding area E. Ciampino has few restaurants and shops, but a couple of cafes are open until 9pm.

DUTY FREE & CUSTOMS REGULATIONS

Duty free If you're travelling to/from a non-EU country you may carry a maximum of 200 cigarettes, 1L of alcohol with 22% ABV or more, or 2L of alcohol below 22% ABV.

Cashed up If you plan to enter or leave the EU with more than €10,000 (or equivalent) in cash, you must declare it to customs. If you don't, authorities may hold the cash and fine you.

GETTING TO THE CITY CENTRE

From Fiumicino Leonardo Express runs to Termini every 15 minutes (30 minutes, €14). Regional trains (€8) travel to Roma Trastevere (30 minutes) and Roma Tiburtina (50 minutes). Public buses (€2.80) run to main metro stations from Terminal 1; Terravision and Sit Bus Shuttle go to Termini (€7) from Terminal 3. TAM Shuttles (€10) run all night to Termini and Ostiense.

From Ciampino No direct train to the city. Ciampino Airlink bus-train shuttle (€2.70) goes to Termini. Atral buses go to Anagnina metro (20 minutes, €1.20); bus 720 runs to Laurentina metro (€1.50). Terravision and Sit Bus Shuttle go to Termini (€6, 40 minutes).

HOW MUCH FOR A...

train €14 30 minutes

bus €2.80 one hour

taxi €50 30 minutes

Taxi A taxi from Fiumicino/Ciampino to the historical centre costs €50/31. These are fixed prices for any location inside the Aurelian Walls.

Left luggage Fiumicino has a storage facility (€10 per item for 24 hours) in Terminal 3, open 7am to 11pm.

Private shuttles Many companies offer private transport from the airports to any address in the city. These are especially convenient for groups, who can have a driver wait for them at arrivals for as little as €10 per person. Book online with Fiumicino Airport Shuttle (fiumicino airportshuttle.com) or Welcome Pickups (www.welcomepickups.com/rome).

OTHER POINTS OF ENTRY

Trains to Termini The largest train station in Italy connects to most major cities in the country. Regional trains are the cheapest solution when it comes to rail travel, but they're also the slowest. Fast trains such as Le Frecce or Italo reach Rome from Bologna, Florence, Milan, Naples or Venice in just a few hours. Book ahead at trenitalia.com or italotreno.it to get the best prices.

Buses to Tiburtina Long-distance buses from all over Europe, including Flixbus coaches, arrive at Rome's Tiburtina station, in the northeastern part of the city. The Tiburtina metro is approximately 100m from the bus station, connecting you to the rest of the city.

Ferries to Civitavecchia In the town of Civitavecchia, 80km north of the city on the Tyrrhenian coast, daily ferries go to Sardinia and Sicily, and also Barcelona and Tunis. Directferries.it provides detailed information on routes and prices. Civitavecchia's train station is 2km from the port. From there you can reach Termini in less than 1½ hours (€4.60).

TRANSPORT TIPS TO HELP YOU GET AROUND

METRO
Lines A, B, B1 and C connect 74 stations from 5.30am to 11.30pm (1.30am Friday and Saturday).

BUS
ATAC buses run 24 hours to every corner of the city. The main hub is in Termini.

TAXI
White Roma Capitale taxis are officially licensed and can be booked by calling 06 06 09. You'll also find plenty of taxis in Largo Torre Argentina, Piazza Venezia and Piazza dei Cinquecento. The fixed start fee is €3 during weekdays, €4.50 during holidays and €6.50 at night. Always check that the meter is on and working; avoid prearranged fares.

For wheelchair users, the 3750 private taxi company offers an accessible mobility service. Call 06 37 50 to book a ride with one of the vans from its fleet.

€1.50 for 100-minute ticket

FREE

Kids under 10 travel free

See atac.roma. it for real-time updates

WALKING
Walking is the best way to explore the historical centre, especially in the back alleys, where motorised traffic is prohibited.

TRAIN
Some parts of the city are easier to reach with regional and urban trains. Tiburtina, Ostiense, Trastevere and San Pietro stations are among the largest after Termini.

CAR SHARE
Carsharingroma, Car2Go, Share'N'Go and Enjoy offer car-sharing services. Prices range from €0.24 to €0.29 per minute.

SCOOTER SHARE
Electric scooters are everywhere in Rome. Rent via apps like Bird, Lime, Helbiz or Wind. Prices start at €0.15 per minute.

TRAM The tram network has six lines, running 5.30am to midnight daily.

ACCESSIBILITY

Not all public transport is accessible; about 80% of buses (carrying the International Symbol of Access) have ramps, but these vehicles can't be recognised from a distance. On the Metro B line, all stations provide access for travellers with disabilities except Circo Massimo, Colosseo and Cavour. On the Metro A line, only Valle Aurelia and Cipro Musei Vaticani stations offer such access.

PUBLIC TRANSPORT ESSENTIALS

MyCicero app Tickets can be purchased and validated via MyCicero. Connect it to your credit card and plan your journey in a few taps. Alternatively, you can text 'BIT' to 48018 to buy a ticket with your phone.

Buy tickets in advance If you don't use MyCicero, tickets must be bought in advance at stations, automatic machines or *tabacchi* and validated once you start the ride. Checks are infrequent, but you'll be fined €54.90 if you're caught without a ticket.

Tickets and passes You can use the same ticket on bus, metro and tram. A single BIT ticket (€1.50) is valid for 100 minutes from validation. A 24/48/72-hour pass costs €7/12.50/18. A seven-day CIS pass costs €24. Unlimited rides on

public transport are included in the Roma Pass (romapass.it), which gives free or discounted access to tourist sites for 48 (€32) or 72 (€52) hours.

Cycling With intense traffic, cobblestone streets and hills, Rome has traditionally not been great for cyclists. But cycle paths are expanding: there are plans to build 150km of paths in coming years. The Tiber path (pictured above), running through the city for nearly 35km, is the longest. The Aniene path goes from Villa Ada to Ponte Nomentano (4km) and the path from Ponte Risorgimento to Villa Ada (2.6km) runs through the greenery of Villa Borghese.

SAFE TRAVEL

Rome is a safe city. Its major risks are the same as those of any large tourist destination: pickpockets and street scams. These are easily avoided with some care. When in a crowd, keep your eyes open and your belongings close.

THEFT Pickpockets mostly target tourist hotspots and crowded buses that run between large attractions, such as the infamous bus 64 that goes to the Vatican. Protect your valuables and avoid standing by the doors. In case of theft, you can file a report at any police or *carabinieri* (military police) station.

FAKE ATTRACTION TICKETS It is common to see people standing around the Colosseum trying to sell tickets to the archeological park, promising to let you skip the lines or offering a discounted price. Needless to say, there is no guarantee that these tickets are valid. Buy online at parcocolosseo.it or via official channels only.

SCAMS Scammers can get very creative when it comes to stealing money from tourists. Fake charity petitions are common, and so are people pretending to have a gift for you, which will quickly translate into a request for cash.

CHECK FOR PRICES
Avoid entering restaurants and bars where prices aren't shown on the menu or buying services where the cost isn't stated in advance. The same goes for taxis: always make sure the meter is working.

PHARMACIES In each neighbourhood at least one pharmacy – recognisable by a green cross – is open 24 hours on any given day. Ask for *farmacia di turno* if you need to purchase medication at night.

FILIPPO GIULIANI/SHUTTERSTOCK ©

MCLITTLE STOCK/SHUTTERSTOCK ©

EMERGENCIES For all emergencies call 112. This number is free to call from any phone and will connect you to an operator that will redirect you to the appropriate authorities.

COVID-19 HOTLINE
You can reach the official COVID-19 hotline by calling 1500. You'll be answered by an operator from the Ministry of Health. The number is free to call and staffed 24/7.

QUICK TIPS TO HELP YOU MANAGE YOUR MONEY

CREDIT CARDS Major credit and debit cards (Visa, Mastercard) are accepted by nearly every commercial enterprise. By law, businesses in Italy must have a POS system to accept electronic payments. Some smaller shops might frown upon receiving small payments by card, but the option should always be available.

TIPPING
Tipping is optional in Italy. You can leave a *mancia* (tip) if you feel like it by rounding up the bill.

SAVE MONEY: GO PLASTIC-FREE
The Waidy WOW app helps you find water fountains in Rome, mapping the *nasoni* where you can fill your bottle for free.

CURRENCY

Euro

HOW MUCH FOR...

an espresso
€1

a gelato
€2.50

a margherita pizza
€7

COPERTO O SERVIZIO?

For decades it was common for Italian restaurants to levy a *coperto* (cover charge). In 2006 a law was introduced forbidding businesses to do so. Some restaurants simply changed the name of the fee to *servizio* (service charge). While this applies at a minority of businesses, you may be charged extra (€1.50 to €2 per person) for service. In most cases, the fee is stated on the menu.

COFFEE AT THE BAR
Do as Italians do: drink your espresso standing up at the bar. If you choose to sit down you might be charged a service fee.

CHANGING MONEY
Banks offer exchange services only to customers. Unless you have an Italian bank account, you must rely on money changers, which are concentrated around Termini.

VAT REFUND
Non-EU citizens spending at least €154.95 in shops displaying a 'Tax-Free' sign are entitled to a VAT refund ranging from 11.6% to 15.5% of the purchase amount.

ATMS *Bancomat* (ATMs) are scattered all around the city. Commissions for withdrawing cash can be costly. Exchange rates at ATMs tend to be reasonable, although there's a withdrawal limit (usually €250).

RESPONSIBLE TRAVEL

Positive, sustainable and feel-good experiences around the city

CHOOSE SUSTAINABLE VENUES

Eat to support refugee integration The Gustamundo restaurant has operated in Via Giacinto de Vecchi Pieralice since 2017, hiring migrants and political refugees to promote integration through stories and diverse culinary traditions. @@gustamundo_roma

Buy fair-trade, organic goods Visit the Sunday market of the 3500-sq-metre event space Città dell'Altra Economia in the Testaccio neighbourhood – one of the first spaces in Europe dedicated to the promotion of an alternative economy.

Look out for Slow Food products The Slow Food organisation promotes projects and products that protect genuine traditions and local ecosystems. Seek out restaurants recognised by Slow Food's guide to support the region's biodiversity and the people who care about it. @@slowfoodroma

GIVE BACK

Buy produce cultivated on lands confiscated from the Mafia Look out for the Libera Terra label when shopping for groceries at places such as NaturaSì.

Learn about social struggles Visit Città dell'Utopia – a volunteer-run organisation at Via Valeriano 3F – to participate in talks, movie screenings, games, and courses on topics such as gender inequality, the environment and social inclusion.

Donate or volunteer to help the homeless Binario95 (binario95.it), located by Termini, has been providing a home for the homeless for the past 20 years. Do your part by donating or participating in volunteering events.

SUPPORT LOCAL

Shop at markets Support small vendors while enjoying the lively atmosphere of one of Rome's many markets. Testaccio, Porta Portese, Esquilino, San Lorenzo – it's your choice.

Search for unique souvenirs at bottegas Whether it's handmade shoes or a carved picture frame, you'll never be disappointed by the quality at Roman artisans' workshops.

LEARN MORE

Learn about lesser-visited neighbourhoods Go beyond the centre and explore the culture of Garbatella on a walking tour by Unexpected Rome, run by local architect and certified guide Valeria Castiello. @unexpectedrome

Discover the city's multicultural character Learn about the rich history of Esquilino by joining a walk by Migrantours (mygrantour.org).

Enjoy farm-to-table vegetarian dishes Reduce your footprint and discover delicious traditional dishes (made with hyperlocal ingredients) at Il Margutta (Via Margutta 118).

LEAVE A SMALL FOOTPRINT

Reduce food waste Download the app Too Good to Go to get unsold food from eateries at a discounted price.

Shop at zero-waste stores Buy packaging-free groceries at Negozio Leggero (Via Chiabrera 80) or Resto Sfuso (Via Santa Maria Ausiliatrice 68).

Drink plastic-free Visit fontanelle.org to locate a nearby drinking fountain (the city has 5000) to refill your bottle.

ROME POSITIVE-IMPACT TRAVEL

CLIMATE CHANGE & TRAVEL

It's impossible to ignore the impact we have when travelling, and the importance of making changes where we can. Lonely Planet urges all travellers to engage with their travel carbon footprint. There are many carbon calculators online that allow travellers to estimate the carbon emissions generated by their journey; try resurgence.org/resources/carbon-calculator.html. Many airlines and booking sites offer travellers the option of offsetting the impact of greenhouse gas emissions by contributing to climate-friendly initiatives around the world. We continue to offset the carbon footprint of all Lonely Planet staff travel, while recognising this is a mitigation more than a solution.

RESOURCES
cittadellaltraeconomia.org
slowfoodroma.it
lacittadellutopia.org
toogoodtogo.org

UNIQUE AND LOCAL WAYS TO STAY

While sleeping in the historical centre is more expensive than anywhere else in the city, Rome's accommodation prices are in line with those of any European capital. A variety of options are available, from hotels with mesmerising views on the city's main piazzas to tranquil private residences tucked away from the crowds.

Find a place to stay in Rome

HOW MUCH FOR A NIGHT IN...

a central hotel
€120

a hostel dorm
€25

an Airbnb/private apartment
€100

HERITAGE BUILDINGS

Many heritage buildings formerly used by governmental institutions have been transformed into unique hotels. The most recent example is the Bulgari Hotel, set to open in 2022 in the monumental Palazzo dell'INPS in Piazza Augusto Imperatore.

VIEWS, VIEWS, VIEWS

Every major square has at least one hotel with a spectacular view. Admire Rome's rooftops from the terraces of Les Etolies, Palazzo Montemartini or Pantheon Iconic Rome.

BUDGET-CONSCIOUS STAYS

Rome isn't just palaces and high-end chains. Hostels such as RomeHello and Generator offer beds in a fun atmosphere at prices as low as €25 per night.

CASTLE SOJOURNS

Head out of the centre for a truly unmatched experience. Sleep in one of the many medieval castles surrounding Rome.

BOOKING & TAXES

Many hotels offer deals or discounts if you book directly through their official websites.

Prices rise during the high season (April to June, September and October), while good deals can be found in August and from November to February.

Ecobnb (ecobnb.it) This booking platform rates hotels, apartments and glamping spots based on ecofriendliness.

Taxes A tourist accommodation tax is charged within the borders of Rome's municipality. The tax ranges from €3 per day for budget stays to €7 per day for five-star hotels.

PARKING

If you're travelling by car and your hotel doesn't offer parking, use the MyCicero or EasyPark app to find parking spots and pay fees.

WHERE TO STAY, IF YOU LOVE...

Archaeology and iconic ruins Ancient Rome (p30) The Colosseum, the Forum and the Palatine are just waiting to be discovered.

Vintage shopping, design and street art Monti, Esquilino & San Lorenzo (p112) Close enough to the major sights, with independent brands, bookshops and design stores.

Monumental fountains, good coffee and art Tridente, Trevi & the Quirinale (p74) Toss your coin in the Trevi Fountain, then move on to the wonderful Palazzo Barberini to admire baroque art.

Street art and industrial architecture Southern Rome (p174) Neglected by most visitors, Ostiense, surrounding the towering Gazometro, expresses its character through giant wall art and cosy cafes.

Market vibes and local life San Giovanni & Testaccio (p142) The best traditional Roman food, served in the authentic atmosphere of residential Testaccio, south of the centre.

↓ Parks, romantic atmosphere and art Villa Borghese & Northern Rome (p158) Villa Borghese offers a masterpiece-filled gallery surrounded by lush greenery.

↑ Religion, ceiling frescoes and awe-inspiring architecture Vatican City, Borgo & Prati (p96) Long lines may be a drag, but there's a reason seven million people visit the Vatican Museums every year.

Sculpture, churches and bars Centro Storico (p52) Home to vibrant bars and restaurants, and close to museums holding exceptional art, the magnificent Piazza Navona is justifiably crowded.

High-end shopping and dining Tridente, Trevi & the Quirinale (p74) Glossy Tridente is home to all major brand names.

Nightlife, cafes and views Trastevere & Gianicolo (p126) Surrounded by bars, restaurants and *aperitivo* spots, and walking distance from ancient Rome, Trastevere is fun, but noisy until late.

Unexpected flavours and Jewish heritage Centro Storico (p52) By the Tiber, the Jewish Ghetto is home to ancient traditions best discovered through the cuisine.

ESSENTIAL NUTS-AND-BOLTS

GREETINGS
On informal occasions, people greet each other by giving a light kiss on both cheeks. If you're unsure what to do, follow the other person's lead.

SPLITTING THE BILL
In Italy, *fare alla romana* (doing it the Roman way) means splitting the bill equally among all members of a group.

LUNCH BREAK
Many stores close between 1pm and 4pm to allow workers to take a lunch break.

FAST FACTS

Time Zone
GMT+1

Country Code
+39

Electricity
230V/50Hz

GOOD TO KNOW

Visitors from 62 non-EU countries can travel to Italy for tourism without a visa for up to 90 days.

Validate train tickets before you enter the train and bus tickets after you enter the bus.

By law, cash payments are limited to a maximum of €2000.

Dinner is usually eaten between 7.30pm and 9pm.

A cappuccino is considered a breakfast drink. Stick to espresso after 11am.

ACCESSIBLE TRAVEL

Visiting historical attractions The Colosseum (which has a lift), the Vatican Museums, the Capitoline Museums, St Peter's Basilica and the Pantheon are all accessible to wheelchair users.

Y&Co app The official Y&Co app features itineraries through ancient Rome designed for blind or vision-impaired visitors and deaf or hearing-impaired visitors.

Cobblestone streets and absent footpaths The uneven streets of Rome's historical centre can be hard to navigate in a wheelchair, and footpaths can be narrow or nonexistent.

Larger hotels These are your best bet when it comes to accessibility. Avoid booking small B&Bs or private apartments unless you are sure of their accessibility status.

OUTFIT ETIQUETTE

Cover up when visiting churches (no tank tops and no shorts) and dress up to dine out.

DIGITAL NOMADING

To work on your laptop, use a co-working space (€10 to €15) rather than a cafe.

PUBLIC TOILETS

Cafes expect you to buy something to use their facilities. Public toilets usually cost €1.

FAMILY TRAVEL

Bus rides are free for all children under 10.

Everyone under 18 can enter the Colosseum, the Forum and the Palatine Hill for free.

For a break from archaeological sites visit the Explora Children Museum, where kids can test their skills with hands-on craft workshops and scientific experiments.

The Al Sogno toy store in Piazza Navona will take you back in time amid hundreds of old-school, artisanal carillons, stuffed animals and dolls.

STREET DRINKING

Drinking on the street is technically legal in Italy, although local laws can limit what is allowed. At the time of writing, shops could not sell take-away alcohol between 10pm and 7am and street drinking was prohibited between 11pm and 7am in 14 areas of Rome.

SMOKING

Smoking is prohibited in enclosed public spaces, including restaurants, shops and public transport. There's an exception for bars that function as private clubs and require membership. To prevent fires, it's forbidden to smoke in public parks such as Villa Borghese and Villa Ada in summer.

LGBTIQ+ TRAVELLERS

Discrimination is uncommon, but negative episodes still occur. Gay couples have reported being called out on public transport in recent months, and the Church's influence on the city's culture remains strong.

Via di San Giovanni in Laterano, steps from the Colosseum, is the beating heart of Rome's LGBTIQ+ scene.

Rome's Gay Pride takes place in June, with celebrations starting in Piazza Vittorio Emanuele II. Visit romapride.it for the full program.

Arcigay (arcigay.it) is the largest Italian LGBTIQ+ nonprofit organisation.

218

 LANGUAGE

When in Rome, you'll find that locals appreciate you trying their language, no matter how muddled you may think you sound. Italian is not difficult to pronounce as the sounds used in spoken Italian can all be found in English.

Note that, in our pronunciation guides, ai is pronounced as in 'aisle', ay as in 'say', ow as in 'how', dz as the 'ds' in 'lids', and that r is a strong and rolled sound. Keep in mind too that Italian consonants can have a stronger, emphatic pronunciation – if the consonant is written as a double letter, it should be pronounced a little stronger. The Italian ch is is usually pronounced as a hard c, so, for example, 'chiesa' is 'key-esa'.

BASICS

Hello.	*Buongiorno.*	bwon·*jor*·no
Goodbye.	*Arrivederci.*	a·ree·ve·*der*·chee
Yes./No.	*Sì./No.*	see/no
Please.	*Per favore.*	per fa·*vo*·re
Thank you.	*Grazie.*	*gra*·tsye
Excuse me.	*Mi scusi. (pol)*	mee *skoo*·zee
	Scusami. (inf)	*skoo*·za·mee
Sorry.	*Mi dispiace.*	mee dees·*pya*·che

What's your name?
Come si chiama? (pol)   *ko*·me see *kya*·ma
Come ti chiami? (inf)   *ko*·me tee *kya*·mee

My name is ...
Mi chiamo ...   mee *kya*·mo ...

Do you speak English?
Parla/Parli   *par*·la/*par*·lee
inglese? (pol/inf)   een·*gle*·ze

I don't understand.
Non capisco.   non ka·*pee*·sko

TIME & NUMBERS

What time is it?	*Che ora è?*	ke o·ra e
It's one o'clock.	*È l'una.*	e *loo*·na
It's (two) o'clock.	*Sono le (due).*	*so*·no le (*doo*·e)
Half past (one).	*(L'una) e mezza.*	(*loo*·na) e *me*·dza
in the morning	*di mattina*	dee ma·*tee*·na
in the afternoon	*di pomeriggio*	dee po·me·*ree*·jo
in the evening	*di sera*	dee *se*·ra
yesterday	*ieri*	*ye*·ree
today	*oggi*	*o*·jee
tomorrow	*domani*	do·*ma*·nee

1	*uno*	*oo*·no	6	*sei*	say
2	*due*	*doo*·e	7	*sette*	*se*·te
3	*tre*	tre	8	*otto*	*o*·to
4	*quattro*	*kwa*·tro	9	*nove*	*no*·ve
5	*cinque*	*cheen*·kwe	10	*dieci*	*dye*·chee

EMERGENCIES

Help!	*Aiuto!*	a·*yoo*·to
Leave me alone!	*Lasciami in pace!*	la·sha·mee een *pa*·che
Call the police!	*Chiami la polizia!*	*kya*·mee la po·lee·*tsee*·a
I'm lost.	*Mi sono perso/a. (m/f)*	mee *so*·no *per*·so/a

Index

000 Map pages

THIS BOOK

Design development
Lauren Egan, Tina Garcia,
Fergal Condon

Content development
Anne Mason

Cartography development
Wayne Murphy, Katerina
Pavkova

Production development
Mario D'Arco, Dan Moore,
Sandie Kestell, Virginia
Moreno, Juan Winata

**Series development
leadership**
Liz Heynes, Darren O'Connell,
Piers Pickard, Chris Zeiher

Commissioning Editor
Sandie Kestell

Product Editor
Saralinda Turner

Cartographer
Alison Lyall

Book Designer
Clara Monitto

Assisting Editors
Sarah Bailey, Michelle
Bennett

Cover Researcher
Lauren Egan

Thanks Gwen Cotter, Karen
Henderson, John Taufa

Our Writers

ELISA COLAROSSI

Elisa is a Roman born and raised freelance travel writer and illustrator. Her knowledge on Roman culture and lifestyle allows her to truly unveil the 'how to' when in the Eternal City, revealing an unforeseen Rome and giving the spotlight to lesser-known neighborhoods.

@romangalgoesaround

My favourite experience is to explore neighbourhoods that are out of the ordinary like Centocelle (where I was born), Quadraro, Pigneto and Alessandrino.

ANGELA CORRIAS

Sardinia-born Angela is a Rome-based travel journalist and blogger and loves writing her blogs about Italy and her international travels. Passionate about culture and lesser-visited destinations, Angela is working on a book about her travels and life in Afghanistan.

@angelacorrias

My favourite experience is strolling around Rome's off-the-beaten-path streets and neighbourhoods to find hidden gems and underground historical sites.

ANGELO ZINNA

Angelo Zinna is a writer and photographer based in Florence, Italy. Passionate about architecture, literature and environmentalism, he is the author of the travelogue *Un Altro Bicchiere di Arak* (VME, 2016) and creator of the podcast Cemento.

@angelo_zinna

My favourite experience is pizza – every neighbourhood has its own stand-out street-food option and seeking them all out is an ongoing adventure.